A BUFFALO SCRAPBOOK

St. Mark Parish

The Loving Legacy of Msgr. Francis Braun and Sr. Jeanne Eberle

By Steve Cichon

A Buffalo Scrapbook: St. Mark's Roman Catholic Parish

© 2014 Buffalo Stories LLC, staffannouncer.com

ISBN 978-0-9828739-2-2

Published by Buffalo Stories LLC and staffannouncer.com

All Rights Reserved

Introduction

Since people found out I was writing this book, many have been asking excitedly when my history of St. Mark is coming out. I have had to politely correct them.

I learned the hard way that writing "the history" of anything is nearly impossible. Learning, uncovering, and sharing the people, places, and events which make us who we are today is always a living, breathing, on-going adventure. Collating and curating over a thousand of pages worth of memories, photos, stories, and news clippings into a book is not an end point, but a fresh beginning to dig even further.

Nearly a decade ago, I set out to collect and write "The Complete History of Parkside," which I proudly published in 2009. I now jokingly refer to that 174 page book as "The Almost Complete History of Parkside," because the stories, photos, and information I've become privy to since the printing of that book could easily fill two more volumes of the same size.

That is why I call this book-- and every book I now write-- a "scrapbook," and not a "complete history."

Through years of listening to and recording stories and hour upon hour of research, my goal has always been to uncover the great stories of St. Mark and its people. It's my hope that as you read these pages and look at the photos included here, that you are also reminded of great stories of our parish and its people which didn't happen to make it into this work. It's my further hope that you'll share those stories, photos and memories with me and others, so that the next St. Mark scrapbook adds yet another layer to the recorded history of our beloved parish and school.

Dedication

To Msgr. Francis Braun and Sr. Jeanne Eberle

From a St. Mark School yearbook

How blessed we would be, as a community, to have had 30 years of leadership and love from a single, wonderful person of God who cared about each of us as much as this person cared about our wonderful parish.

Someone who offered us an example of living a Christ-like life based in giving everything of themselves and asking nothing in return.

The Loving Legacy of Fr. Braun and Sr. Jeanne

Of course, we'd be blessed to have had one such person in our lives and the life of our parish... But how extraordinarily blessed are we to have had two such pillars of our community?

Sr. Jeanne Eberle and Msgr. Francis Braun: Often different in their manner, but very similar in their tireless work, dedication, and love.

How incredibly blessed the entire St. Mark community and each of us individually have been to have their light and love in our lives.

We could fill a whole shelf of books with the tales of the selfless giving, extraordinary encouragement, and seemingly bottomless numbers of extra hands lent by Father and Sister in times of need.

It was a very special and pure love which flowed from our rectory and convent, and it's a love we'll always feel, as we know it continues for each one of us and our community to this day.

So, Fr. Braun and Sr. Jeanne--

We love you, too. Saying thank you doesn't feel like enough, but thanks for helping to make our parish what it is, and each of us who we are as individuals.

Thank you, too, for continuing to provide a wonderful Christ-like example in our ever-hardening world.

And most of all, thanks for the love, support and friendship which has left an indelible mark on thousands of lives in North Buffalo and beyond.

A Buffalo Scrapbook: St. Mark's Roman Catholic Parish

NEW CATHOLIC CHURCH IN CENTRAL PARK DISTRICT

Bishop Colton Appoints Well Known Young Priest to New Parish.

Announcement has just been made by Bishop Colton of the formation of a new parish in the Central Park section of this city. The Rev. Father John J. McMahon, pastor of Our Lady of Mt. Carmel Church on Fly and La Couteulx Streets, has been assigned by the Rt. Rev. Bishop to undertake the organization of the new mission and the building of the new church. The appointment is regarded as a well-deserved promotion for this popular and efficient young priest.

The decision of Bishop Colton to establish a church in this locality will be hailed with delight by the Catholic population of the Central Park section, and the news of Father McMahon's appointment will be equally pleasing to them. On account of the great distance to the nearest Catholic church, the people of that faith living in the Central Park section have been greatly inconvenienced in getting to church on Sunday.

It is expected that a magnificent church will be erected as soon as Father McMahon and his new parishioners decide upon a suitable site. The limits of the new parish extend on the west side of Main Street from Florence Street to Hertel Avenue and west, approximately, to Delaware Park and the Niagara Boulevard. It is one of the rapidly growing sections of the city and one that will amply support this new parish.

Father McMahon is well known to Buffalo people as one of the most successful young priests of the diocese. With the exception of a short assignment to Jamestown and one year spent as assistant superintendent of parochial schools, most of his priestly labors since his ordination in Rome in 1900 have been in this city. Two and one-half years ago Father McMahon was appointed pastor of the new Italian Church on Fly Street, and in this difficult charge he has acquitted himself with the greatest credit. A harmonious parish of over 10,000 persons, a well-equipped school of nearly 700 pupils and a thoroughly purified district are some of the features of Father McMahon's work in the lower section of Main Street. No successor to Father McMahon has yet been announced.

The Loving Legacy of Fr. Braun and Sr. Jeanne

SAINT MARK ROMAN CATHOLIC CHURCH was

founded on June 25, 1908 by Bishop Charles H. Colton, D.D., who also appointed Rev. John J. McMahon, then pastor of Our Lady of Mt. Carmel Church on Fly Street in the Canal District, as the pastor of the new parish.

At the time of its founding, Catholics in the new parish had been members of either St. Vincent de Paul on Main Street just north of Fillmore Avenue, or St. Joseph on Main Street north of Winspear Avenue.

Thirty-five Catholic families made up the original parish roster. Many early parishioners were servants in the stately homes of the new and rapidly growing Central Park and Parkside neighborhoods, which together made up most of the parish.

Hertel Avenue was the northern boundary, with Florence Avenue to the south. Main Street to the east, with Delaware Park and the Niagara Boulevard (now Colvin Avenue) to the west.

The area was rapidly growing, but not the fully developed city neighborhood known today. A history of St. Mark's written for the parish's 40th anniversary notes that "pioneer parishioners state that, in the early days of the parish, much of the parochial territory was so thinly settled and so rustic in appearance that one could stand on Russell Avenue and observe, through the trees, the street cars on Hertel Avenue."

While completing a census of the Catholics in the area, raising money, and finding a suitable location to build a church, Fr. McMahon lived in an apartment at 25 Russell Avenue.

Eventually, four lots were purchased on Woodward Avenue, and a wooden frame church was built where St. Mark School now stands. The building with room for 252 people cost $2250 completely furnished. Bishop Colton celebrated the first Mass on September 6, 1908, less than nine months after the establishment of the parish. A wood and stone rectory was built in 1910.

Opposite page: Buffalo Courier, 1908.

The first St. Mark Church, circa 1910 with the stone rectory in the foreground and Rev. John McMahon standing on the walkway. The church stands in about the area occupied by the parking spots in front of the most northern entrance to the school. The photo below shows the same two buildings, straight on. Notice the houses visible on the other side of Summit Avenue.

BISHOP COLTON DEDICATES CHURCH

Impressive Ceremony at Consecration of St. Mark's Edifice.

NEW PARISH IN PARKSIDE DISTRICT

The new Roman Catholic Church of St. Mark's, in the Parkside and Central Park districts, was formally dedicated by the Right Rev. Charles H. Colton yesterday, when the Rev. John J. McMahon, formerly of Our Lady of Mt. Carmel, was installed as rector. The ceremonies attendant on the dedication began at 10 o'clock in the morning and were participated in by prominent clergy, including the Right Rev. Nelson H. Baker, vicar general of the diocese; the Right Rev. P. J. Cannon, of Lockport; the Rev. Dr. John D. Biden, rector of St. Joseph's Cathedral; the Rev. Dr. J. J. Nash, pastor of the Holy Family Church; the Rev. Father Grill, of St. Vincent's; the Rev. L. F. Sharkey, of St. Lucey's, and the Rev. Christopher O'Byrne, of St. Nicholas.

The blessing of the sacred edifice by the bishop in accordance with the ritual of the church, was followed by solemn high mass, celebrated by Father McMahon, assisted by the Rev. Patrick Gilmour, deacon; the Rev. D. J. Mountain, sub-deacon, and the Rev. Dr. J. Hennessey, master of ceremonies.

Following the first gospel of the mass Bishop Colton preached an eloquent and impressive sermon, congratulating pastors and people on the auspicious opening of a new church in the Parkside district. The people were felicitated on the selection of the new parish, which takes in much of the territory formerly comprised in the parishes of St. Vincent's and St. Joseph's, both in Union Street, but at a considerable distance from each other. The right reverend prelate specially commended his hearers the teachings of the great evangelist, St. Mark. In closing he predicted a happy future for the new parish and expressed the hope that the new rector would receive the cordial support of every true Catholic in the district.

During the celebration of the mass Father McMahon extended a welcome to the bishop, priests and friends who had honored the occasion by their presence. For his congregation there assembled for the first time, he had a special greeting thanking one and all for the royal reception and generous encouragement attending his advent among them. He announced the appointment of the following trustees of St. Marks: George Leonard of Crescent Avenue, and Henry Benson, of Vernon Place. The hours of service next Sunday will be 8 and 10 o'clock in the morning.

The Gregorian mass sung by the choir, was under the able direction of Thomas M. Cronyn, the hymn, "Ecce Sacerdos Magnus," sung as the bishop entered the church, being especially well rendered. Mrs. P. J. Quinn, organist of Our Lady of Mt. Carmel, efficiently presided at the organ. The ceremonies concluded with the benediction of the Most Blessed Sacrament by Bishop Colton, and the singing of the "Te Deum" by the choir.

On June 25 Bishop Colton established the new parish and assigned Father McMahon. Ground was broken immediately thereafter and in the short space of four weeks the new church, a modest frame building, handsomely furnished and accommodating about 300, was completed. Within a few years it will be succeeded by a larger and more imposing edifice, as the district is growing rapidly.

Buffalo Courier 1908

A Buffalo Scrapbook: St. Mark's Roman Catholic Parish

Notice the somewhat rural looking surroundings as Bishop Colton lays the cornerstone of the current St. Mark Church, August 16, 1914.

By 1914, 254 families were members at St. Mark, and the cozy 252 person wooden church was busting at the seams at Mass time.

On August 16, 1914, the cornerstone was laid for a new Indiana limestone church at the corner of Amherst Street and Woodward Avenue, and the building was completed the following year.

The early Gothic style building, designed by A.A. Post, cost $59,000. People of the time marveled at the fact that unlike most other churches of its size, St. Mark had no columns to support the ceiling.

From the original church, remain the Italian marble statues of the Blessed Virgin Mary, St. Joseph, the Sacred Heart of Jesus, and St. Anthony. The main and side altars of the current church are made from the same fine marble. The pews, pulpit and confessionals were crafted from quarter-sewn white oak, the ceiling paneled in chestnut, and the Stations of the Cross were imported from France.

Much of the rest of St. Mark's artistic appointments were the work of the Roman-trained Panzironi Brothers of New York City. The family of artisans has been active in the creation of artwork in churches since the sixteenth century in Florence, Italy. Ilario Panzironi, who was most likely the primary artist of the 5 murals surrounding the altars of St. Mark, was knighted by Pope Pius XI in 1926.

St. Mark's.

The interior of the church has been beautifully decorated by an Italian artist. The grounds adjoining the rectory have been graded and grass seed sown and will soon be in keeping with the beauty of the surroundings.

Last Sunday the children received their first holy communion. Previous to the reception of the sacrament, Father McMahon addressed them, telling of the great love of Jesus for little children. He spoke of the supreme happiness that was theirs and congratulated them on their faithful and earnest preparation and advised them to receive frequently and regularly. After mass the children, 25 in all, renewed their baptismal vows and were enrolled in the scapular.

On Monday night our Rt. Rev. Bishop administered the sacrament of confirmation and spoke to the large assemblage of the necessity of the sacrament in order that our faith might be strengthened by the gifts of the Holy Ghost. He congratulated pastor and parishioners on the splendid work accomplished, on the continuous growth of the parish and the many improvements made since his last visit. After confirmation benediction was given by Bishop Colton, assisted by Rev. Thomas J. O'Hern, Father Zimmerman, Father O'Byrne, Father Sharkey and Father McMahon.

A Buffalo Scrapbook: St. Mark's Roman Catholic Parish

Above: Nearing the end of construction of St. Mark church, 1915. Below: St. Mark is celebrated upon completion in the Buffalo Courier.

BEAUTIFUL NEW CHURCH ERECTED IN CENTRAL PARK DISTRICT—ST. MARK'S

The illustration shows the new St. Mark's Catholic church at Amherst street and Woodward avenue, which was formally occupied by pastor and congregation on Sunday, May 30. The new edifice is of bluish-grey Indiana limestone, its architecture being after the quaint style of the Fourteenth century English gothic, peculiarly adaptable to the high and beautiful Central park district, in which the church is a new ornament as well as convenience. The church was designed and its erection directed by Architect Albert A. Post. The building is 155 feet in length, the breadth of nave is 54 feet and of transept 65 feet, and the structure is 56 feet in height. The interior ceiling is paneled in chestnut wood. The pews are built of quartered oak, the floor ing of tile and the whole interior finish, principally in oak, gives a restful and artistic effect. The view of the sanctuary is unobstructed there being no pillars in the auditorium and his people erected the new St. Mark's at an expenditure approximating $75,000.

DEDICATION OF NEW ST. MARK'S IS IMPRESSIVE

Bishop Dennis J. Dougherty Officiates at Ceremonies Assisted by Distinguished Clergymen — Characterizes Church as Model for Others.

Saint Mark's church, at Woodward avenue and Amherst street, was dedicated by the Rt. Rev. Dennis J. Dougherty yesterday forenoon, in the presence of a large congregation and a distinguished gathering of clergymen. Bishop Dougherty, in cope and miter, sat on an episcopal throne at the left of the sanctuary during the celebration of solemn mass by the pastor, the Rev. John J. McMahon.

A guard of honor, chosen from the men of the parish, met the bishop on his arrival at the rectory and escorted him to and from the church.

Assisting Father McMahon in the mass were: the Rev. John C. Carr of Saint Francis de Sales church, deacon; the Rev. Charles A. Maxwell of Saint Lucy's church, sub-deacon; the Rev. Dr. Thomas J. Walsh, chancellor of the diocese, first master of ceremonies; the Rev. Leo Toomey of Saint Joseph's cathedral, second master of ceremonies.

The Rev. Henry R. Laudebach of Saint Louis church and the Rev. William Schreck of Saint Gerard's church were chanters; Gerald Gleason, processional cross bearer; Francis Kelsey, book bearer; Paul Hens, miter bearer; Robert Reinhart, holy water bearer; Arthur Adams, Richard Reinhart, Robert Kinkade, James Freitas, Harry Freitas, Louis Hartman, Gordon Gannon, Raymond Murray, George Gardiner, Irving Farrell, Clement Drexelius, acolytes. William Walsh, organist, directed Saint Mark's choir of 20 voices in a special program.

Bishop Dougherty was attended by the Rev. Michael A. Irwin of Saint Marks' church, Newton Grove, N. C., assistant priest; the Rev. James F. McGloin of Saint Joseph's cathedral and the Rev. John J. Roche of Holy Angels' church, deacons of honor.

Congratulates Parishioners.

Congratulating pastor and parishioners on their progress, Bishop Dougherty said the history of Saint Mark's was typical of the growth of the Catholic church in the United States.

"In 1790 Bishop Carroll reported 20,000 Catholics in the United States; there are 20,000,000 Catholics in this country and the priests number 20,000. Natural increase of the Catholic family, unrestricted by artificial means, is the first cause of this growth; the second is the influx of immigrants reared in Catholic belief; the third is conversions, estimated by experts to number 100,000 a year."

Characterizing the new Saint Mark's edifice as a model, in artistry and accommodations, for other churches, Bishop Dougherty said: "Under God, undoubtedly the greatest credit for this work is due to the late and dearly beloved Bishop Colton." Next to him in the bishop's appreciation, came Saint Mark's pastor and parishioners because of their zeal, labors and sacrifices. Especial gratitude was expressed to donors of windows, side altars and interior furnishings and the anonymous giver of the main altar, "an artistic gem."

The church was not formally dedicated until two years after it was in use, following the death of Bishop Colton in 1915.

A Buffalo Scrapbook: St. Mark's Roman Catholic Parish

Rev. John J. McMahon

Pastor of St. Mark 1909-1928

Bishop of Trenton, NJ, 1928-1932

The Loving Legacy of Fr. Braun and Sr. Jeanne

The Rev. John J. McMahon was the first pastor of St. Mark Parish. In 1908, he started with little more than an area carved out of two neighborhood parishes, and a few dozen families willing to help build a community.

Over his twenty years as pastor, Fr. McMahon oversaw the building of the first church, the rectory, the current church, the bell tower, and the school.

As explained in the text of the parish's 50th Anniversary booklet, "one of the great blessings of St. Mark's is that everything Fr. McMahon did from the very beginning was conceived in quality and dignity." He made sure the buildings he built and the furnishings with which they were furnished were of the highest quality, and meant to last for generations.

John J. McMahon was one of nine children born to Margaret and Martin McMahon in Hinsdale, New York.

After graduating from St. Bonaventure in 1895, he joined the seminary there. After a competition, he completed theology studies in Rome, and was ordained at St. Peter's Basilica in 1900. Through his travels, education, and various assignments, he became fluent in Latin, Greek, Hebrew, Spanish, French, German, and delivered sermons in twenty different Italian dialects during his career.

After serving as Superintendent of Catholic Schools in Buffalo, he was named Pastor of Our Lady of Mount Carmel Church in "The Hooks" section of Buffalo near the terminus of the Erie Canal and Buffalo Harbor.

Two years later, Fr. McMahon came to North Buffalo and St. Mark where he'd remain for two decades.

As pastor at St. Mark, he continued to travel the world, spending months away visiting Rome and places like the Panama Canal, always bringing back perspective and stories for not only his parishioners, but the Diocese of Buffalo at large.

A Buffalo Scrapbook: St. Mark's Roman Catholic Parish

THE REV. JOHN J. M'MAHON.
Pastor of St. Mark's Church, who was welcomed home by his parishioners.

PARISHIONERS GREET FATHER M'MAHON ON RETURN FROM EUROPE

Four hundred parishioners of St. Mark's Church greeted the Rev. Father John J. McMahon, last night, upon his return from a four months' trip to Europe. It was an evening of great rejoicing for the congregation and the popular priest was gratified beyond expression at the magnificent reception accorded him.

Father McMahon arrived from New York early in the evening and was met at the station by a men's committee headed by William A. King. After being entertained at dinner at the Iroquois Hotel, he was escorted to the rectory in Woodward Avenue. The parochial residence was decorated with flags and a big electric sign, bearing the words, "Welcome Home" adorned the front door.

When the committee entered the residence they were greeted by 400 happy parishioners each of whom gave Father McMahon a personal welcome and, in addition, Henry Benson delivered an address and presented the pastor with a purse of gold. A number of other gifts were presented. The women of the parish gave a table, desk and rocking chair, Mrs. A. J. Post making the presentation. Father McMahon responded feelingly, thanked the parishioners for the welcome, and said that he was glad to be among his people again.

The parishioners also remembered Father Mullins who has filled the pastorate during Father McMahon's absence. He was presented with a purse and other gifts.

POPE CONFERS SIGNAL HONOR ON FATHER M'MAHON

St. Marks' Church Pastor Receives Autographic Rescript from His Holiness—Gift a Surprise.

The Rev. John J. McMahon, pastor of St. Mark's church, Woodward avenue and Amherst street, has been slightly favored in the receipt of an autographic rescript from his Holiness, Pope Benedict XV, in which the holy father through a papal decree composed in his own handwriting and sent directly from the vatican to Father McMahon, personally sends not only the papal blessing to the esteemed pastor of St. Mark's and the people of his parish, but also adds one of the greatest gifts which the holy father may confer, a plenary indulgence to be communicated through Father McMahon to his parishioners upon the occasion of the formal dedication of the new St. Marks church, soon to take place.

The letter, which will be carefully preserved among the archives of the new parish, came to Father McMahon as a complete surprise through the instrumentality of the Very Rev. Alexis M. Lepicier of Rome, a former professor of Father McMahon when a student 19 years ago in Rome.

Now Prior General.

Father Lepicier is now the prior general of the order of the Servites of Mary throughout the entire world, and naturally stands very high in ecclesiastical circles in the Eternal City, as is evidenced by the fact that Pope Benedict XV granted him an audience sought especially for the purpose of informing His Holiness of the services of Father McMahon in the diocese of Buffalo as pastor of several important parishes, especially in the Church of Mount Carmel in this city, where Father McMahon had charge of the largest Italian parish in the city, and lastly of his great work in building up the now successful parish and church of St. Mark's.

Father McMahon anounuced yesterday to his people the signal blessing which the Holy Father had conferred upon them and himself. As a result Father McMahon was the recipient of many congratulations from his parishioners and friends because of the distinguished favor which had come to him.

The special envoy of the Holy Father to the United States, Most Rev. John Bonzano, was to have officiated at the dedication of St. Mark's church, May 30, but the death of Bishop Colton intervened, and the formal dedication had to be deferred until a new bishop is appointed.

CELEBRATES 25TH ANNIVERSARY AS PRIEST WEDNESDAY

The Rev. John J. McMahon Long Prominent in Buffalo Diocese.

The Rev. John J. McMahon, pastor of St. Mark's Roman Catholic church, will celebrate the twenty-fifth anniversary of his ordination to the priesthood Wednesday.

He was graduated with high honors from St. Bonaventure's college at Allegany with the degree of bachelor of arts in 1895. In 1906 following a competitive examination he was chosen by the Rt. Rev. P. J. Cannon Bourse for the celebrated Urban College of the Propaganda, Rome Italy. Completing his course at this pontifical institution, he graduated with a degree of bachelor of sacred theology and was ordained to the priesthood in the Eternal city in the jubilee year of 1900, May 20.

School Executive

After he returned to the United States he was made assistant superintendent of parochial schools under Bishop Gibbons, when the latter was superintendent of the Buffalo parochial schools. He was the first non-Latin priest to be made pastor of an Italian congregation in the Buffalo diocese, the appointment being made by the late Rt. Rev. Charles Henry Colton, D. D., to the parish of Our Lady of Mt. Carmel. There he built up a large parish and opened the largest Italian parochial school in the diocese in February 1906.

June 25, 1908, he was directed to found the now flourishing parish of St. Marks, Woodward avenue and Amherst street. Under his administration it had become one of the leading parishes in the city and diocese.

St. Mark's Rector 25 Years in Priesthood

THE REV. JOHN J. McMAHON.

The property and buildings consist of a magnificent stone church of Gothic architecture. There is a spacious and up-to-date parochial school and rectory. Royal blue Indiana limestone was used in construction of all the buildings. The property is valued at $575,000.

The church and school were blessed and dedicated by Bishop Turner. After Bishop Turner's advent to Buffalo, Father McMahon was made first master of ceremonies of the diocese, which position he held at the time of Bishop Gibbon's and Bishop Walsh's consecration and Bishop Turner's installation as Bishop of Buffalo, in St. Joseph's new cathedral.

Six years ago Father McM hon was made director of the diocesan paper, well-known throughout the United States, the Catholic Union & Times. He was also chosen as diocesan director of the Holy Name

A Buffalo Scrapbook: St. Mark's Roman Catholic Parish

Solemn Blessing of Saint Mark's Parish School
BY
RT. REV. WILLIAM TURNER, D. D.
Bishop of Buffalo

Rev. JOHN J. McMAHON, LL. D., Pastor   Rev. MARTIN B. FELL, Assistant

October 16, 1921

Menu

BLUE POINTS

Saltines   Olives   Celery

CHICKEN BOUILLON WITH RICE
Salt Sticks

ONE-HALF BROILED SPRING CHICKEN
Whole Browned Potatoes   Peas

French Rolls   Sherbet   Heart of Lettuce—French Dressing   Cheese Straws

FRENCH VANILLA ICE CREAM

Cake   Almonds   Mints

CIGARS   COFFEE

SERVICE BY KOCHER'S, 2500 MAIN STREET

The Loving Legacy of Fr. Braun and Sr. Jeanne

More than 50 "prominent Catholic clergymen" were on hand as St. Mark School was dedicated on October 16, 1921. From that date until the retirement of Sr. Jeanne Eberle, the education of the children of St. Mark's had been under the care and supervision of the Sisters of St. Joseph.

The building was equipped with "an up-to-the-minute gymnasium, physical culture room, bowling alleys, and domestic science facilities." The Buffalo Express called it "the equal of any modern school building its size in the city."

At the time the school was dedicated, there were 275 families in the parish. That's almost nine times the number of families which made up St. Mark when it as founded thirteen years earlier.

From a 1940's history of the parish: On May 25, 1925, after a High Mass, a record attendance of parishioners marched in procession to the spacious lawn before the school, where a metal flagpole and large American flag were blessed. Mr. Martin Phillips, an alumnus of Canisius College and Georgetown University, delivered a stirring address on "The Parochial School and American Patriotism." The large flag was then raised as all present pledged their allegiance to God and country. Fr. McMahon then addressed the assemblage and gave his blessing.

A Buffalo Scrapbook: St. Mark's Roman Catholic Parish

Scene at the consecration of the new bell in Saint Mark's church, Woodward avenue and Amherst street, Sunday afternoon. The sermon was delivered by Monsignor Nelson H. Baker, left. The Rev. Father John J. McMahon, pastor of the church, at right.

Buffalo Evening News photo from inside St. Mark Church. More than 60 priests gathered to dedicate the parish's new bells and eighty-eight foot bells tower.

In June, 1924, Msgr. Nelson Baker presided over the consecration and blessing of the new angelus bells and bell tower dedicated to the newly created Feast of Christ the King.

The Loving Legacy of Fr. Braun and Sr. Jeanne

St. Mark, 1926 as appeared in the Buffalo Courier at the time of the bell tower dedication.

A Buffalo Scrapbook: St. Mark's Roman Catholic Parish

Newly Consecrated Bishop of Trenton

This picture shows the Rt. Rev. John J. McMahon, D. D., Catholic bishop of Trenton, N. J., as he entered St. Joseph's cathedral for his consecration Thursday morning. The Rt. Rev. Edward F. Gibbons, D. D., bishop of Albany, is shown in the background.

After 20 years as pastor of St. Mark Church, Pope Pius XI named Rev. John McMahon the Bishop of Trenton, New Jersey. Fr. McMahon was consecrated a bishop on the Feast of St. Mark in 1928.

The Loving Legacy of Fr. Braun and Sr. Jeanne

FATHER M'MAHON BECOMES BISHOP

Twenty-eight Years of Labor Crowned With Recognition at Colorful Service in Cathedral.

Twenty-eight years of labor as a priest in the Buffalo diocese were crowned with recognition Thursday morning in St. Joseph's cathedral, Delaware avenue and West Utica street, when the Rt. Rev. John J. McMahon, pastor of St. Mark's church, Amherst street and Woodward avenue, was consecrated bishop of the Roman Catholic diocese of Trenton, N. J.

In an impressive ceremony, the Rt. Rev. William Turner, bishop of Buffalo, pronounced the words which made Bishop McMahon a prelate of the church.

An archbishop and four bishops took part in the consecration. Bishop Turner was consecrator, assisted by the Rt. Rev. Thomas J. Walsh, newly-appointed bishop of Newark, N. J., and the Rt. Rev. Edmund F. Gibbons, bishop of Albany, both former Buffalo priests.

Succeeds Bishop Walsh.

Bishop McMahon succeeds Bishop Walsh in the Trenton diocese. Bishop Walsh was chancellor of the Buffalo diocese before his elevation to the bishopric. Bishop Gibbons is a former superintendent of parochial schools here, and was assisted by Bishop McMahon for some years.

The Most Rev. John T. McNicholas, archbishop of Cincinnati, O., preached the sermon. The Rt. Rev. Thomas J. Shahan, bishop of Washington, D. C. also assisted at the ceremony.

Led by nearly 100 priests of the Buffalo diocese, the episcopal procession moved from the chapel of the Blessed Sacrament into the cathedral under the gaze of hundreds who had gathered to witness the ceremony. The cathedral was crowded.

Laymen's Delegation Here.

Many out-of-town clergymen were present. A delegation of Catholic laymen from Trenton, N. J., headed by Vincent J. Bradley, president of the New Jersey Real Estate board, was on hand for the consecration of their new prelate. Bishop McMahon will be installed in Trenton on May 10.

The new bishop's consecration fell on the feast of St. Mark, patron saint of the parish which he founded in 1908. A special indult of the pope was necessary to comply with Bishop McMahon's wish. Ordinarily, bishops are consecrated only on a Sunday or on the feast of an apostle.

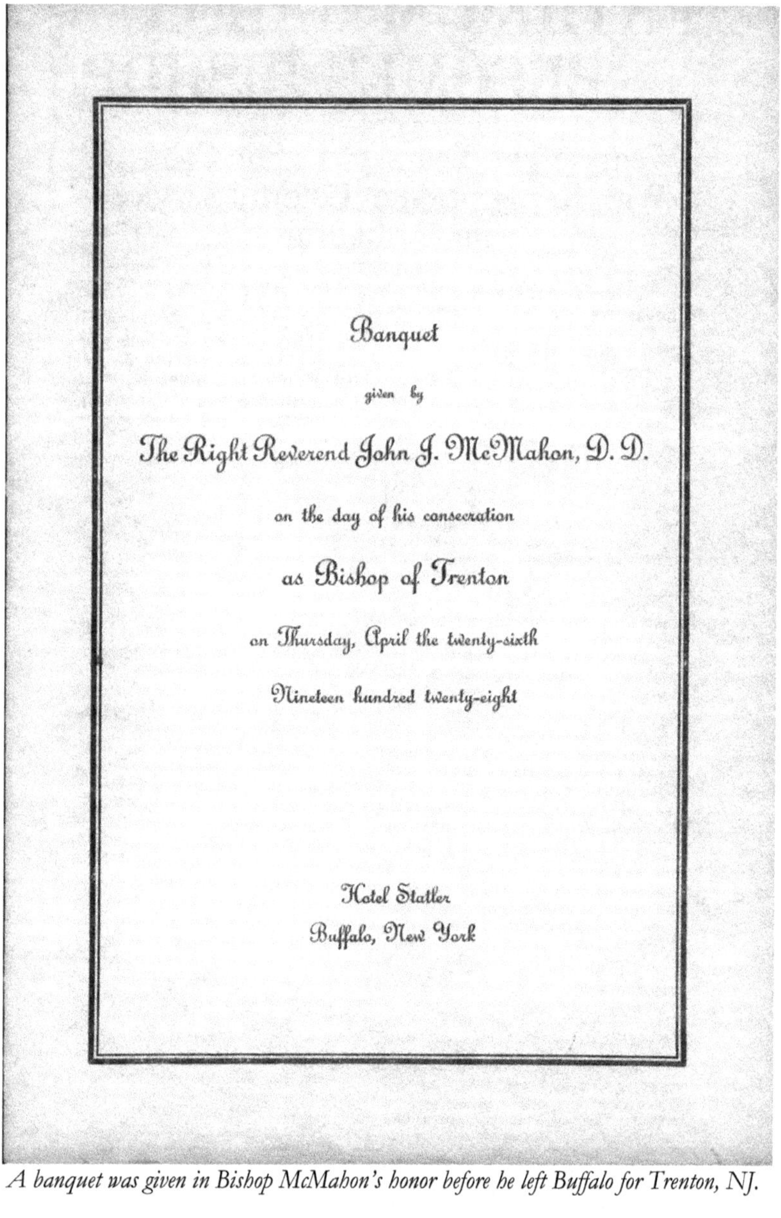

Banquet

given by

The Right Reverend John J. McMahon, D. D.

on the day of his consecration

as Bishop of Trenton

on Thursday, April the twenty-sixth

Nineteen hundred twenty-eight

Hotel Statler
Buffalo, New York

A banquet was given in Bishop McMahon's honor before he left Buffalo for Trenton, NJ.

His Excellency,
Most Reverend John Joseph McMahon, D. D.
Bishop of Trenton --- First Pastor of St. Mark's

A Buffalo Scrapbook: St. Mark's Roman Catholic Parish

Bishop M'Mahon Resumes Duty as Pastor of Church

Celebrates Mass in St. Mark's as Before Consecration, to Continue Routine Until Departure May 9.

The rich pomp and pageantry that accompanied his elevation to the bishopric Thursday, was but a memory Friday morning, when the Rt. Rev. John J. McMahon, bishop of Trenton, N. J., said the 8 o'clock mass for his parishioners at St. Mark's church, Amherst street and Woodward avenue, just as he had done for eight years as their pastor.

Despite all the ceremony of the preceding day that marked the consecration of the Buffalo pastor as bishop of Trenton, he resumed the routine of St. Mark's Friday, as if there had been no interruption. He will continue to say the 8 o'clock mass daily and attend to other duties attached to the pastorate, until May 9, when he will leave for Trenton to be installed.

To Say Children's Mass.

Sunday Bishop McMahon will say the 9 o'clock children's mass, and at that time they will receive holy communion from his hand. He also will impart the episcopal blessing.

Bishop McMahon will be a guest at a number of dinners given in his honor by ecclesiastical and lay organizations. He will be honored by the Holy Name society at a dinner at 6 o'clock Sunday evening, May 6. The place where the dinner will be served has not been decided on.

Bishop McMahon will say a pontifical mass in St. Mark's church, Sunday, May 6. A temporary throne has been erected in the sanctuary and a plaque bearing the episcopal coat of arms has been hung over it.

Many Dignitaries Leave.

Many dignitaries who attended the consecration departed Thursday night. The rest left Buffalo Friday. The Rt. Rev. Thomas J. Walsh, bishop of Newark, and formerly of Buffalo, returned to his see Thursday night. Bishop Edmund F. Gibbons of Albany, formerly of Buffalo, left Buffalo Friday.

Eleven priests and more than 400 monsignori and priests, including 80 from the Trenton diocese, were guests of the Rt. Rev. John J. McMahon at a banquet in the Hotel Statler Thursday afternoon, following his consecration. The Rev. Luke F. Sharkey, pastor of St. Brigid's church, was toastmaster.

Speakers paid tribute to Bishop McMahon's character and achievements and predicted a brilliant success for him as head of the Trenton diocese. The new bishop was extolled as a model priest, one whose talents and virtues are not demonstrative but which, it was said, are strongly felt.

Bishop Tells of Pope.

Responding to the toast, "Our Holy Father," the Rt. Rev. William Turner, bishop of Buffalo, told of the pope's knowledge of conditions in this diocese, revealed on Bishop Turner's audiences with him during the last visit of the Buffalo prelate to Rome. The loyalty of the Buffalo diocese was pledged by Bishop Turner as a tribute of obedience, submission and love to the Holy See.

Toasting the diocese of Buffalo, the Rt. Rev. Edmund F. Gibbons, D.D., bishop of Albany, eulogized the memories of Bishops Colton and Ryan and expressed grateful remembrance of his own years in Buffalo. He described the welcome which Trenton gave to the Rt. Rev. Thomas J. Walsh, bishop-elect of Newark, whom Bishop McMahon succeeds, and predicted that the new bishop will be received with similar enthusiasm.

Bishop Walsh Praises Parish.

Bishop Walsh expressed his delight at having Bishop McMahon as successor and, in the name of the Trenton diocese, pledged the co-operation of the priests and laity for their new bishop. There is not a more prosperous diocese in the United States than Trenton, Bishop Walsh said. He extolled the religious spirit of the Catholics of the diocese and tolerance of the Protestant clergy and laymen, and told of a letter received from a Presbyterian minister, head of the Trenton Federation of Churches, expressing a spirit of good will to the new Catholic prelate.

The Very Rev. Thomas F. Plassmann, president of St. Bonaventure's college, expressed the gratitude of the college and its alumni for the luster which he said Bishop McMahon has shed on the name of his Alma Mater. He lauded Bishop McMahon's work as a parish priest and leader of the Holy Name society in the Buffalo diocese. Loyalty Father Plassmann said, is the bishop's outstanding quality.

Thanks Buffalo Priests.

Bishop McMahon thanked the priests of Buffalo for their evidences of affection received Thursday. He especially thanked Bishops Turner, Walsh and Gibbons, and others who assisted in the consecration ceremonies. Express-

---

Relief from Gas Stomach Pains Dizziness

The doctors tell us that 90 per cent of all sickness is due to stomach and bowel troubles. You can't be well if your digestion is bad; you are likely to get sick unless you relish food and digest it properly.

Tanlac has a wonderful record as a relief from digestive troubles, even those of years' standing.

Mrs. Ellen White of 21 Sanger St., New Hartford, N. Y., writes us: "For years I suffered from indigestion. I got no relief from anything until I took Tanlac. After my fourth bottle, I feel like a new person and have a fine appetite."

If you suffer from gas, pains in the stomach or bowels, dizziness, nausea, constipation or torpid liver; if you have no appetite, can't sleep and are nervous and all run down, you need Tanlac. It is good, pure medicine, made of roots, herbs and barks. Get a bottle from your druggist today. Money back if it doesn't help you.

Tanlac
52 MILLION BOTTLES USED

The Rev. Robert E. Walsh succeeded Bishop McMahon as the second pastor of St. Mark. He was ordained in 1898, and arrived in North Buffalo from St. Patrick's Church in Salamanca. A 1954 history called Fr. Walsh "a deeply devout man of stately and dignified appearance." In a final show of love, when Fr. Walsh died in 1937, 250 parishioners accompanied his body on a special Erie Railroad train to Corning where he is buried.

CHURCH ANNIVERSARY

St. Mark's parish to celebrate 25th year

St. Mark's Roman Catholic parish, Woodward Avenue and Amherst Street, will celebrate the 25th anniversary of the founding of the parish in a series of events the week of October 15th.

The parish was established in 1908 when the late Bishop John J. McMahon was assigned by the late Bishop Colton to organize the church unit. The Parkside district then was only sparsely settled, but signs were evident of the growth to come and the head of the diocese appointed Father McMahon to the task. The young priest who later became bishop of the diocese of Trenton, N. J., met with sixteen men, residents of the district, and the first steps were taken to acquire the property on which the church, school and rectory now stand.

A temporary wooden church was erected and the first mass was celebrated in the new church the second Sunday in October in that year. Five years later the present structure was completed and opened for services.

The anniversary program includes a pontifical high mass Sunday, October 15th, a parish banquet the following evening and a card party, Thursday, October 19th. Archie W. Ralyea is chairman of the banquet committee and William J. Flynn is chairman of the committee arranging the card party.

1933 booklet commemorating St. Mark's 25th Anniversary:

It is with sentiments of deepest gratitude to Almighty God, that St. Mark's Parish this year, nineteen hundred thirty-three, celebrates its Silver Jubilee.

A Buffalo Scrapbook: St. Mark's Roman Catholic Parish

ST. MARK'S TO OBSERVE 25TH ANNIVERSARY

Pontifical high mass tomorrow will initiate series of events

Ushering in the first in a series of events in celebration of the 25th anniversary of the founding of the parish, pontifical high mass will be sung in St. Mark's Roman Catholic Church, Woodward Avenue and Amherst Street at 10.15 o'clock tomorrow morning.

Bishop William Turner will occupy the episcopal throne in the sanctuary and will be attended by the Rev. Robert E. Walsh, now pastor of the parish, as arch priest, and Msgrs. Joseph Gambino and Richard O'Brien. Officers of the mass will be: Msgr. John J. Nash, celebrant; the Rev. Francis Garvey, deacon, and the Rev. Raymond Murray, subdeason. Msgr. Edmund J. Britt will be master of ceremonies and the Rev. Fancis Hendricks will be assistant mastor. of ceremonies. The Very Rev. Thomas Plassman, O. F. M., president of St. Bonavanture's College, will preach the sermon.

The mass will bring together many former parishioners and a special effort has been made to have in attendance the living members of the original group of sixteen men who formed the parish in 1908 when the late Bishop John J. McMahon was assigned as the first pastor.

More than 400 reservations have been made for the parish banquet which will be held in the parish auditorium Monday evening. William J. Flynn will be toastmaster and the principal speaker will be Judge Thomas H. Dowd of Salamanca. Others who will speak are Paul J. Batt, John V. Maloney, Martin Phillips and William Brennan, Jr. On Thursday evening a card party will be held in the auditorium.

Silver Jubilee Program

Sunday, October 15, 1933 -- Bishop's Day

10:30 A. M.—SOLEMN MASS 'CORAM EPISCOPO'

Celebrant	Rt. Rev. Msgr. John J. Nash, D.D.
Deacon of the Mass	Rev. Francis Garvey
Sub-Deacon of the Mass	Rev. Raymond Murray
Arch-Priest	Rev. Robert E. Walsh
Assisting Deacons	{ Rt. Rev. Msgr. Joseph Gambino { Rt. Rev. Msgr. Richard O'Brien
Master of Ceremonies	Rt. Rev. Msgr. Edmund J. Britt
Ass't Master Ceremonies	Rev. Francis P. Hendricks
Thurifer	Rev. John Shea

Monday, October 16, 1933 -- Parish Day

9:00 A. M.—SOLEMN HIGH MASS for Living and Dead of the Parish

Celebrant	Rev. Robert E. Walsh
Deacon	Rev. Martin Fell
Sub-Deacon	Rev. David J. Mullins
Master of Ceremonies	Rev. Francis Garvey

7:00 P. M.—BANQUET

Toastmaster—MR. WILLIAM J. FLYNN

Speaker—HON. JUDGE THOMAS H. DOWD (Salamanca)

Toasts:

Rt. Rev. Msgr. Edmund J. Britt	Our Holy Father
Mr. John V. Maloney	Our Flag
Mr. Martin G. Phillips	Our Men
Mr. William Brennan, Jr.	St. Mark's Ladies
Mr. Paul V. Batt	St. Mark's School
Mr. Charles G. Duffy	Former Parishioners

From the 1933 booklet commemorating St. Mark's 25th Anniversary:
Blessed in the keen foresight and sound judgment of that priestly priest and Bishop, Father McMahon, first pastor; blessed in piety, the generosity and loyal cooperation of a faithful flock, St. Mark's now pauses to give expression to those feelings of heartfelt thanks to Him Who is the Giver of "every best and every perfect gift."

A Buffalo Scrapbook: St. Mark's Roman Catholic Parish

Abandoned in St. Mark's Church

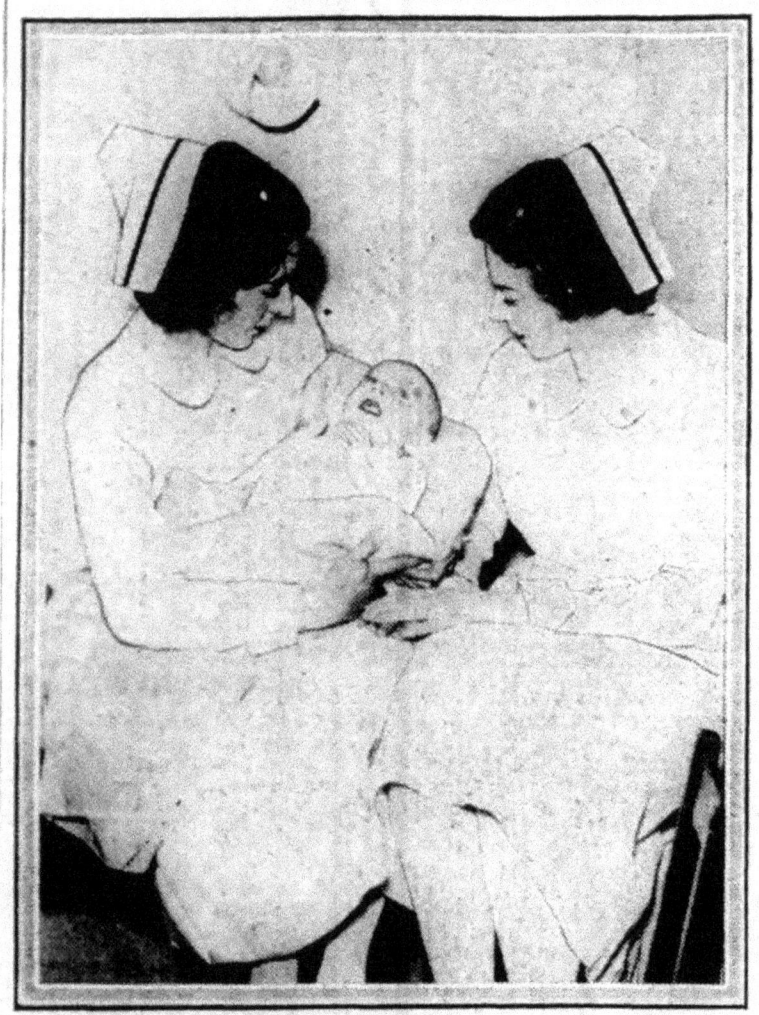

Appropriately, this little fellow is likely to bear the given name Mark if his parents are not found. He is shown here in the City Hospital, in the care of Evelyn MacDonald (left) and Phyllis Bannister.

The Loving Legacy of Fr. Braun and Sr. Jeanne

Find Boy, Three Months Old, In Pew of Church

Abandoned infant attracts attention with cries; taken to City Hospital

A crying blue-eyed baby boy was found abandoned at 7.30 o'clock last night in a rear pew of St. Mark's Church, 405 Woodward Avenue, at Amherst Street. Confessions, which were in progress, were interrupted by a shrill cry and several women who were present found the youngster in a pew, lying on a blanket.

Attached to the blanket was a card which read: "Born January 7th." Thus the baby was abandoned exactly three months after the day it was born. Also lying on the blanket was a bottle containing cod liver oil, a feeding bottle, a powder bottle and a thermos bottle containing warm milk.

The child wore a white bonnet and cloak and a pink woolen overshirt. He was tidy.

The Rev. Robert Walsh, pastor of St. Mark's Church, notified the police and Patrolmen Arthur J. Van Remmen and Adolph Dickman of the radio scout car division took him to the City Hospital. Hospital authorities said that the child was in good health.

The Rev. Father Walsh and the women present said that the child should be named Mark, since he was found in St. Mark's Church. He may assume that name if the parents are not found.

PLAN PARISH SOCIAL

Church folk to hold function Wednesday evening

Parishioners of Holy Name of Jesus Church, Bailey Avenue, are making preparations for the card party and social to be held in the new auditorium of St. John Kanty's Lyceum, Broadway and Swinburne streets, Wednesday evening. They are endeavoring to make this party one of the most attractive ever sponsored by the parish.

Pedro, auction bridge and rhummy will be played. More than 200 gifts will be presented to winners. Cards begin at 8 o'clock.

Following the card party a social will be held. Joe Armbruster's Orchestra will play for dancing.

Card Party and Dance

A public card party and dance will be held in the Polish Falcons Hall, Crane Street, Depew, this evening. Casimir Cybulski, president, is chairman.

lation is necessary for the Falls to proceed. The state health department, however, take the position that to be on the safe side, enabling legislation should be enacted at this session.

In 1934, during the throes of The Great Depression, a three month old baby boy was left in the pews of St. Mark during confession. No further information was published on the case.

A Buffalo Scrapbook: St. Mark's Roman Catholic Parish

Fr. Walsh with students of St. Mark

St. Mark's Church Society
FINANCIAL STATEMENT
Feb. 1, 1932 to Feb. 1, 1933

RECEIPTS		EXPENDITURES	
Cash on Hand	$ 27.13	Pastor	$ 1,200.00
Pew Rent	3,810.00	Assistants	2,200.00
Offertory	9,473.78	Teachers	2,470.00
Monthly	7,654.75	Organists	940.50
Fuel	878.70	Janitor	1,784.80
Tower Collection	1,585.75	Other Help	1,748.00
Devotions and 40 Hours	614.88	Insurance	738.67
Shrines	1,234.47	Coal	2,050.14
O. S. V.—Commonweal	253.97	Light	599.35
Book Rack	27.45	Taxes	613.14
Parish Societies	1,553.13	Telephone	95.83
Thank Offering	3,172.00	Water	82.10
Candles and Easter	448.25	Interest	3,300.00
Bowling Party	108.15	Mortgage	8,000.00
Propagation of Faith	170.25	Printing	347.11
Little Seminary	214.00	Charity	287.25
Indian and Negro	55.00	General Expense	608.07
Holy Land	24.00	Church Repairs	1,303.08
Seminary	150.00	School and Hall	1,065.34
Holy Father	150.00	House	52.34
Catholic University	128.20	Societies	484.32
National Catholic Welfare	30.00	Book Rack	142.61
		Diocesan	740.45
Total	$31,763.86	C. Union Store	371.29
Cash to Balance on Hand	$ 388.59	Altar Breads	200.88
		Total	$31,375.27

REV. ROBERT E. WALSH,
Pastor, Treasurer and Trustee.

REV. FRANCIS GARVEY,
REV. FRANCIS HENDRICKS,
Assistants.

MR. HENRY J. BENSON,
MR. JOHN BOLAND,
Trustees.

Baptisms 26   Marriages 9   Deaths 33

Above: St. Mark's numbers at a glance in 1933.

Next page: In the early years, even during the Depression, every parishioner's offering to the parish was published and distributed in a quarterly report. One of six pages of the 1930 report is printed over the next two pages.

A Buffalo Scrapbook: St. Mark's Roman Catholic Parish

ST. MARK'S COLLEC

1930

AMHERST STREET

#	Name	Jan Church	Jan School	Feb Church	Feb School	Mar Church	Mar School	Tower
1078	Mr. and Mrs. J. Creahan	1.00		1.00		1.00		3.00
1078	The Misses Creahan	1.00	1.00	1.00	1.00		2.00	6.00
1372	Mr. and Mrs. R. E. Burger	4.00	4.00	4.00	4.00	4.00	4.00	6.00
1376	Mr. and Mrs. W. E. Mahar	1.00	1.00	1.00	1.00	1.00	1.00	3.00
1376	Miss J. Hanavan	1.00	1.00	1.00	1.00	1.00	1.00	3.00
1461	Mrs. H. E. Brade	1.00		1.00		1.00		
1508	The Misses Benson	2.00	1.00	2.00	1.00	2.00	1.00	3.00
1580	Mr. A. Gingras	1.00		1.00		1.00		
1700	Mr. Conrad May	1.00		1.00		1.00		3.00
1702	Mr. and Mrs. Edward May	1.00	1.00	1.00	1.00	1.00	1.00	2.00
1707	C. Speich			1.00	1.00			
1709	Mr. Frank Downey	1.00						
1711	Mrs. R. J. Anthony	1.00		1.00				
1711	Mr. and Mrs. J. R. Doyle	1.00	1.00	1.00	1.00	1.00	1.00	
1714	Dr. W. Knittel		.50		.50			
1735	Mr. and Mrs. F. J. Keating	1.00	1.00	1.00	1.00	1.00	1.00	
1741	Mr. and Mrs. Murphy			1.00	1.00			

BEARD AVENUE

#	Name	Jan Church	Jan School	Feb Church	Feb School	Mar Church	Mar School	Tower
48	Mrs. John Kinney	3.00	2.00	3.00	2.00			
91	Mr. and Mrs. E. J. Lutz			2.00	2.00	2.00	2.00	6.00
91	Edmund J. Lutz	1.00	1.00	1.00	1.00	1.00	1.00	
100	Mr. and Mrs. Thomas V. Ray	5.00	5.00	5.00	5.00	5.00	5.00	
116	Mr. and Mrs. George J. Kreuz	2.00	2.00	2.00	2.00	2.00	2.00	
116	Mr. George P. Kreuz			1.00		1.00		
147	Mr. and Mrs. W. J. Flynn	3.00	2.00	3.00	2.00	3.00	2.00	7.50
150	Joseph M. Conrad	1.00		1.00		1.00		
153	Mrs. C. J. Kast	1.00	1.00			1.00	1.00	3.00
159	Mrs. H. Hoag	2.00		2.00		2.00		3.00
225	Miss Hillery	1.00	1.00	1.00	1.00	1.00	1.00	
225	Mr. and Mrs. W. H. Fitzpatrick	5.00	5.00	5.00	5.00	5.00	5.00	
225	Mr. and Mrs. George Strauss	5.00	5.00	5.00	5.00	5.00	5.00	
325	Mr. John V. Maloney	5.00	5.00	5.00	5.00	5.00	5.00	15.00
229	Mrs. Mary Shea	2.00		2.00		2.00		

COLVIN AVENUE

#	Name	Jan Church	Jan School	Feb Church	Feb School	Mar Church	Mar School	Tower
40	Mrs. Ledra Herman	1.00		1.00		1.00		1.00
65	Mr. and Mrs. Austin Summers	3.00	2.00	3.00	2.00	3.00	2.00	

CRESCENT AVENUE

#	Name	Jan Church	Jan School	Feb Church	Feb School	Mar Church	Mar School	Tower
196	Misses Colmey	1.00	1.00	1.00	1.00	1.00	1.00	
196	Misses Ryan			2.00	2.00	2.00	2.00	1.00
196	Mr. James Whalen			1.00	1.00	1.00	1.00	
216	Mr. and Mrs. C. J. Irwin	7.00	3.00	7.00	3.00	7.00	3.00	
251	Mr. and Mrs. F. Brabant	1.00	1.00	1.00	1.00	1.00	1.00	3.00
251	Mr. P. O. Jacobs	5.00	5.00	5.00	5.00	5.00	5.00	15.00
335	Mrs. B. Mochler			2.00	1.00			
355	Mr. and Mrs. W. F. Wierling	1.00	1.00	1.00	1.00			
360	Misses Marrigan	1.00	1.00	2.00	1.00	1.00	1.00	3.00
362	The Misses Maher			2.00	1.00			
365	J. Carney	1.00	1.00	1.00	1.00	1.00	1.00	1.00
365	Mr. and Mrs. L. H. O'Hara			1.00	1.00			1.00
369	Mr. John Daly	1.00		1.00		1.00		
369	Miss Anna Daly	1.00		1.00		1.00		
378	Mr. and Mrs. R. J. Tresidder	3.00	1.00	3.00	1.00	3.00	1.00	
383	Miss Mary G. Sullivan	2.00	1.00	2.00	1.00	2.00	1.00	
384	Mr. and Mrs. Thomas Kenny	1.00	1.00	1.00	1.00	1.00	1.00	
384	Miss Mary Kenny	1.00	1.00	1.00	1.00	1.00	1.00	
384	Miss Margaret Kenny	1.00	1.00	1.00	1.00	1.00	1.00	
388	Mrs. J. Johnson			1.00	1.00	1.00	1.00	
419	Mr. and Mrs. Joseph M. Kertz	1.00		1.00		1.00		3.00
448	Mr. and Mrs. J. F. Boehm	2.00	1.00	2.00	1.00	2.00	1.00	3.00
448	Mr. Alfred Boehm	1.00	1.00	1.00	1.00	1.00	1.00	3.00
448	Miss Dorothy Boehm	1.00		1.00		1.00		3.00
454	Mr. and Mrs. A. Schwarz	1.00		1.00		1.00		
455	Mr. and Mrs. Thomas E. Carey	1.00	1.00	1.00	1.00	1.00	1.00	
461	Mr. and Mrs. F. D. Cooley	1.00	1.00	1.00	1.00			
464	Mr. and Mrs. Edward Emig	3.00	1.00					
468	Mr. and Mrs. S. V. O'Gorman	1.00	1.00	1.00	1.00	1.00	1.00	
491	Mr. and Mrs. Luke Maxwell	1.00	1.00	1.00	1.00	1.00	1.00	3.00
495	Mr. and Mrs. S. J. Butler	1.00		1.00		1.00		1.00
143	Mr. and Mrs. A. W. O'Brien	1.00	1.00	1.00	1.00	1.00	1.00	
417	Miss Irene Britton	1.00	1.00	1.00	1.00	1.00	1.00	
549	Mr. M. Nielsen	1.00	1.00	1.00				
569	T. J. Bannigan			1.00	2.00	1.00	1.00	
549	Mr. M. Nielsen			1.00	1.00	1.00	1.00	

S CHURCH
CTIONS
1930

CRESCENT AVENUE—Continued

#	Name	Jan Church	Jan School	Feb Church	Feb School	Mar Church	Mar School	Tower
500	Mr. and Mrs. P. C. Dwyer	5.00	5.00	5.00	5.00	5.00	5.00	15.00
501	Mr. and Mrs. W. Tibby	1.00	......	1.00	......	1.00	......	......
506	Mr. and Mrs. Martin Savage	1.00	......	1.00	......	1.00	......	3.00
514	Miss Mary Ennis	1.00	1.00	1.00	1.00	1.00	1.00	3.00
531	Mr. and Mrs. A. H. Spong	1.00	......	1.00	......	1.00	......	1.50
553	F. Elroth	......	......	1.00	......	1.00	......	......
565	Mrs. A. Stanton	1.00	......	1.00	......	1.00	......	3.00
565	Miss Margaret Daly	1.00	1.00	1.00	1.00	1.00	1.00	3.00
567	Miss Mary E. Power	1.00	1.00	1.00	1.00	1.00	1.00	1.00
567	Mr. and Mrs. Harry Williams	1.00	1.00	1.00	1.00	1.00	1.00	3.00
585	Mr. Edward F. Ryan	1.00	1.00	1.00	1.00	1.00	1.00	3.00
597	Mrs. W. M. O'Brien	1.00	......	1.00	......	1.00	......	1.50
597	Miss W. L. Hanrahan	1.00	......	1.00	......	1.00	......	1.50
614	Thomas Ennis	......	......	1.00	......	1.00	......	......
607	Mrs. Clara Hickey	1.00	......	1.00	......	1.00	......	1.05
612	Mr. and Mrs. T. D. Sullivan	1.00	......	1.00	......	1.00	......	3.00
643	The Misses McConnell	1.00	......	1.00	......	1.00	......	1.00
684	Mr. James Lancaster	2.00	2.00	2.00	2.00	2.00	2.00	......
684	Miss Nanette Lancaster	1.00	1.00	1.00	1.00	1.00	1.00	......
690	Mr. and Mrs. Frank Leydecker	1.00	......	1.00	......	......	......	3.00
703	A. McDonald	1.00	1.00	1.00	1.00	......	......	......
706	Miss Martha Gourley	1.00	......	1.00	......	1.00	......	......
706	Miss Katherine L. Gourley	1.00	......	1.00	......	1.00	......	......
707	J. T. O'Connor	......	......	1.00	......	1.00	......	......
741	Mrs. John Kehoe	1.00	......	1.00	......	1.00	......	3.00
762	Mr. and Mrs. E. R. Cooney	2.00	2.00	2.00	2.00	......	......	2.00
772	Miss I. Britton	......	......	......	......	1.00	1.00	......
495	Mrs. Nieman	......	......	1.00	......	......	......	......
743	A. W. O'Brien	1.00	1.00	1.00	1.00	1.00	1.00	......
772	W. S. Fleming	2.00	2.00	2.00	2.00	......	......	2.00
700	Mr. and Mrs. R. E. Ryan	1.00	......	1.00	......	1.00	......	......

DEPEW AVENUE

#	Name	Jan Church	Jan School	Feb Church	Feb School	Mar Church	Mar School	Tower
11	The Misses Nehin	1.00	1.00	1.00	1.00	......	......	......
12	M. P. Morrow	5.00	5.00	5.00	5:00	5.00	5.00	......
38	Mr. and Mrs. Edward H. Kraus	1.00	1.00	1.00	1.00	......	......	......
38	Miss Inez M. Kraus	1.00	......	1.00	......	1.00	......	3.00
109	Paul Batt	2.00	6.00	2.00	6.00	2.00	6.00	......
112	E. J. Garono	5.00	......	5.00	......	5.00	......	7.50
175	Mr. and Mrs. L. Simons	1.00	......	1.00	......	1.00	......	......

EDGE PARK AVENUE

#	Name	Jan Church	Jan School	Feb Church	Feb School	Mar Church	Mar School	Tower
24	Mrs. C. Ianne	1.00	......	1.00	......	1.00	......	3.00

FAIRFIELD STREET

#	Name	Jan Church	Jan School	Feb Church	Feb School	Mar Church	Mar School	Tower
50	Mr. and Mrs. J. Alf	1.00	......	1.00	......	1.00	......	1.50
50	Miss Anne Alf	1.00	......	1.00	......	1.00	......	1.50
58	Mr. and Mrs. Walter Gatt	......	......	1.00	......	1.00	......	2.00
70	Mr. Hubert V. Murray	1.00	......	1.00	......	1.00	......	......
71	Mr. and Mrs. W. Bakos	1.00	......	1.00	......	1.00	......	2.00
76	Mr. and Mrs. J. F. Meidel	1.00	1.00	1.00	1.00	1.00	1.00	......
82	Mr. and Mrs. Terence Haren	1.00	......	1.00	......	1.00	......	......
88	Mr. and Mrs. John Maher	1.00	1.00	1.00	1.00	1.00	1.00	3.00
88	Miss Kathryn Maher	1.00	1.00	1.00	1.00	1.00	1.00	......
104	H. Kelsey	1.00	......	1.00	......	1.00	......	3.00
104	Miss Mary F. Kelsey	1.00	......	1.00	......	1.00	......	2.00
14	Mrs. C. Roberts	......	......	1.00	......	......	......	.50
78	Mrs. Edgar	......	......	......	......	1.00	......	......
104	Miss E. Moynihan	1.00	......	1.00	......	1.00	......	3.00
104	Miss J. Moynihan	1.00	1.00	1.00	1.00	1.00	1.00	3.00
104	E. J. Moynihan	1.00	......	1.00	......	1.00	......	3.00
104	Mrs. C. Moynihan	1.00	......	1.00	......	1.00	......	......

GREENFIELD STREET

#	Name	Jan Church	Jan School	Feb Church	Feb School	Mar Church	Mar School	Tower
25	J. F. Blatner	......	......	1.00	......	1.00	1.00	......
32	Mrs. Henry Adema	5.00	......	5.00	......	5.00	......	6.00
32	Mr. Henry Adema, Jr.	......	......	1.00	......	......	......	......
39	Mr. and Mrs. C. Thompson	......	......	1.00	1.00	......	......	1.00
51	W. E. Maloney	1.00	......	1.00	......	1.00	......	......
53	Miss Irene Murray	1.00	......	1.00	......	1.00	......	1.50
55	Mr. Garrett Fitzgerald	3.00	2.00	3.00	2.00	3.00	2.00	......
60	The Misses Collins	1.00	......	1.00	......	1.00	......	3.00
80	Mr. Michael Roche	1.00	1.00	1.00	1.00	1.00	1.00	3.00
80	Mr. John Roche	1.00	1.00	1.00	1.00	1.00	1.00	3.00
80	Miss Mary Doyle	1.00	......	1.00	......	1.00	......	1.50
80	Mr. Joseph McNamara	1.00	......	1.00	......	1.00	......	......
86	Mr. and Mrs. James Mahoney	1.00	1.00	1.00	1.00	1.00	1.00	......
88	Miss Mary Lynch	1.00	1.00	1.00	1.00	1.00	1.00	3.00

A Buffalo Scrapbook: St. Mark's Roman Catholic Parish

The Right Rev. Charles E. Duffy became the third pastor of St. Mark when Fr. Walsh died in 1937. Msgr. Duffy came from St. Joseph's New Cathedral on Delaware Avenue, where he had served as pastor for eighteen years. Hampered by painful illness during his pastorate, Msgr. Duffy was responsible for many improvements at the church, including the terrazzo floor in the Sanctuary and Sacristy, installing the church's first electronic public address system, and building a pew rent office at the southern end of the church vestibule.

The Loving Legacy of Fr. Braun and Sr. Jeanne

St. Mark's students of the late 1930's and early 1940's

A Buffalo Scrapbook: St. Mark's Roman Catholic Parish

The Loving Legacy of Fr. Braun and Sr. Jeanne

EASTER THRONG—Typical of the throngs attending Buffalo churches yesterday is this scene in front of St. Mark's Roman Catholic Church at Woodward Avenue and Amherst Street as the congregation left the last mass.

The Buffalo Courier-Express captured images of St. Mark parishioners celebrating Easter in 1940 above, and 1941 left.

THE RAIN'S ALL GONE—Coming from mass at St. Mark's Roman Catholic Church, Woodward Avenue at Amherst Street, yesterday morning, Harry Evernden found the unwelcome rain had gone and Sally Landy's umbrella wasn't needed anymore.

A Buffalo Scrapbook: St. Mark's Roman Catholic Parish

The Rev. Joseph A. Burke became the fourth pastor of St. Mark upon the death of Msgr. Duffy in 1942. Within two weeks of his appointment to St. Mark, Fr. Burke was elevated to Monsignor by Pope Pius XII. Five months later, Msgr. Burke was elevated to Bishop, and named Auxiliary Bishop of Buffalo.

The Most Rev. Burke was the pastor of St. Mark for ten years, until in 1952 he became the first local priest named Bishop of Buffalo. He served as Bishop of Buffalo for ten years until 1962, when he died in Rome during the opening of the Second Vatican Council.

Remembered by those who knew him as a warm, personable, giving, and beloved priest, Bishop Burke was born in Buffalo's First Ward to an Irish-native boilermaker father. After attending St. Stephen's School on Elk Street, he became one of the first altar boys at the newly-opened Holy Family Church in 1903.

After attending Canisius High School and College, and studying theology at Innsbruck, Austria, Bishop Burke was ordained to the priesthood in Buffalo in 1912.

His first assignment as a priest of the Buffalo Diocese was as Assistant Pastor at St. Vincent de Paul Church on Main Street near Canisius College, just south of the-then four year old St. Mark Parish. He was also named Confessor to the Nuns at Mt. St. Joseph Academy, just across the street from St. Vincent de Paul at what is now Medaille College.

Fr. Burke volunteered to serve as an Army Chaplain in World War I, and spent several months on the Belgian front. Because of the scarcity of Catholic Chaplains, he remained overseas for nearly a year despite the signing of the Armistice ending the war.

Bishop Burke, along with St. Mark's first pastor, Bishop McMahon, are remembered as St. Mark's bishop pastors in relief artwork on the school auditorium.

Bishop Joseph A. Burke

Pastor of St. Mark 1942-52

Bishop of Buffalo 1952-62

A Buffalo Scrapbook: St. Mark's Roman Catholic Parish

(Photograph by Elizabeth L. Kahle, Courier-Express Staff Photographer)

St. Mark's Has Provided Two Bishops for Church

Father McMahon, Founder of Parish Went To Trenton; Msgr. Burke Waits Consecration

By MARY HELEN O'CONNELL

The parish of St. Mark's has a brief but splendid history. Generously, it has sent two men to wider fields of labor, worthy to bear the dignity of the Apostles of early Christian times.

One, the late Bishop John J. McMahon of Trenton, N. J., was the founder of St. Mark's parish, the other is the Rt. Rev. Joseph A. Burke, native Buffalonian, who last April 20th received the formal announcement of his elevation to the auxiliary bishopric, from the apostolic delegate to the United States, the Most Rev. Amleto G. Cicognani. Bishop-elect Burke will serve as assistant to the Most Rev John A. Duffy and is the first to be appointed in this capacity in the 96 year history of the diocese.

The late Bishop McMahon was graduated from St. Bonaventure's College with high honors and sent to the College of the Propaganda in Rome Italy. After completing his course at the pontifical institution, he was ordained May 20, 1900. Returning to the United States, Father McMahon was made assistant superintendent of the parochial schools of New York State under Bishop Edmund T. Gibbons when the latter was in charge of the schools.

Headed Italian Parish

Father McMahon was the first American priest to be named pastor of an Italian congregation in the Buffalo diocese, having received the appointment from the late Rt Rev. Charles Henry Colton as pastor of Our Lady of Mt. Carmel parish.

It was on June 25, 1908, that Father McMahon formed a new parish in honor of the evangelist, St. Mark The families in the parish numbered 25 when the work of organization began. In the next two years a church, rectory and school were erected under his supervision.

At the installation of the late Bishop William Turner by the late Patrick Cardinal Hayes, Father McMahon was master of ceremonies and as a reward for his distinguished service on that occasion was made diocesan master of ceremonies.

Honored by Bishop

It was Bishop Turner who selected the pastor of St. Mark's as his personal representative and spiritual advisor to the Holy Name Society, an organization which numbered 1,000 members at the time. Under his guidance and because of his keen interest in the movement the enrollment mounted to 24,000.

As founder and pastor of St. Marks, for twenty years, Father McMahon was one of the most scholarly and zealous priests of the Buffalo diocese. During his pastorate the parish of St. Mark's became one of the most important in Buffalo. From its small congregation of 25 families, it increased to include more than 500 families.

On March 7, 1928, Father McMahon was named Bishop of Trenton, N. J., to succeed the Rt. Rev. Thomas J. Walsh, a close friend and a former chancellor of the Buffalo diocese, who had been elevated to the episcopal see of Newark, N. J.

On April 26, 1928, the feast day of the patron saint of the parish he had founded twenty years before, Father McMahon was consecrated by Bishop Turner with Bishops Walsh and Gibbons acting as co-consecrators. His installation in Trenton took place May 10th with Cardinal Hayes presiding at the installation ceremonies. So that his consecration could take place on the feast of St. Mark, a special indult of the Pope was necessary to comply with Bishop McMahon's wish. Ordinarily, bishops are consecrated on a Sunday or on the feast of an apostle.

Bishop McMahon served only a short episcopate before he died December 31, 1933, in Buffalo. His funeral mass here was attended by dignitaries of the church

Continued on Page Two

The Loving Legacy of Fr. Braun and Sr. Jeanne

St. Mark's

Continued from Page One

and high ranking officials in public life. Burial took place in the diocese which he had served, Trenton.

Bishop-elect Burke knows Buffalo and its people because he is a product of Buffalo. He was born here August 27, 1886. His youthful appearance belies his 57 years. He attended parochial schools in Buffalo and was graduated from Canisius High School and College. From 1907 until 1912 he studied at the University of Innsbruck, Austria, and was ordained August 12, 1912, in the Old Cathedral by the late Bishop Charles Henry Colton. His first assignment was at St. Vincent's Church where he served from 1912 until 1918, meanwhile teaching apologetics at D'Youville College. Father Burke enlisted in 1918 and was sent overseas as a chaplain with the rank of first lieutenant. He was on the Belgian front when the Armistice was signed. He served as assistant at the Old Cathedral and for a short time as assistant at the New Cathedral upon his return to the States. He was made pastor of St. Patrick's Church, Fillmore, going to Holy Name of Mary Church, Ellicottville, in 1924. His appointment as pastor of St. Paul's in Kenmore was made in 1932. Father Burke was named pastor of St. Mark's the latter part of 1942 to succeed the late Monsignor Charles E. Duffy. A month after assuming the pastorate of St. Mark's he was created a monsignor.

Colorful Ceremony

The colorful ceremony of consecration will take place Tuesday, June 29th, in St. Joseph's New Cathedral, with Archbishop Cicognani, apostolic delegate to the United States from the Vatican, as consecrator. The ceremony of consecration will be an inspiring and extraordinarily beautiful one. It is a pageant of church ritual that reveals each step of the Christian religion from the days of Christ through the ages which have left their imprint in custom and usage on this ancient ritual. The beautiful scenes of unforgetable splendor will seem like a vivid page from an illuminated volume of past ages. Incense will fill the air and the chants known in the Catacombs will reach a climax when the consecrator lays his hands on Joseph A. Burke and says "Accipe Spiritum Sanctum." Triumphant music and prayer will rend the air when Bishop Burke leaves the Cathedral. In the long history of the Buffalo diocese, Bishop Burke will assume the responsibilities of his position as the fifth diocesan priest named to the Hierarchy of the Church.

Buffalo Courier-Express, 1942
In addition to Bishops Mc Mahon and Burke, St. Mark can also claim Bishop Donald Trautman. The Bishop of Erie from 1990-2012, he was Buffalo's Auxiliary Bishop from 1985-90. Bishop Trautman grew up in North Buffalo and is a graduate of St. Mark.

Tea to Honor Auxiliary Bishop

Mrs. George J. Goetz, president of St. Mark's Guild, is honorary chairman of the annual membership tea to be given next Sunday in the church auditorium. The tea will honor Msgr. Joseph A. Burke, pastor of St. Mark's and auxiliary bishop-elect. — Charlena Smith

St. Mark's Tea Will Honor Msgr. Burke

Mrs. Goetz Chairman For Annual Event

The annual membership tea of St. Mark's Guild will be given from 3 until 6 o'clock next Sunday afternoon in the parish auditorium. The tea will honor the pastor, Msgr. Joseph A. Burke, auxiliary bishop-elect.

Mrs. George J. Goetz, president of the guild, is honorary chairman and Miss Florence Danahy is general chairman. Mrs. Roy W. Lindsay is co-chairman.

Members of the refreshment committee are Mrs. Arthur J. McDonnell and Mrs. Edward J. Quill. Mrs. Edwin A. Munschauer will have charge of the tea table, assisted by Mrs. Arthur P. Skaer, Mrs. George J. Joy, Mrs. John C. Olson, Mrs. Chancey C. Kennedy and Mrs. Walter E. Constantine.

Mrs. Vincent L. Wechter will have charge of the program. In charge of finances for the tea will be Mrs. John W. Johnson and Mrs. Martin J. Littlefield. Invitations for the tea will be the responsibility of Miss Elizabeth Creighton, who will be assisted by Mrs. George C. Lehmann, Mrs. Walter Fleming and Mrs. Frank D. Cooley.

Mrs. Edwin R. Cooney will be in charge of the members who will assist at the urns during the afternoon. Included in the list of assistants are: Mrs. Richard T. Murphy, Mrs. Cornelius J. Hayes, Mrs. Thomas P. Caufley, Mrs. James F. Driscoll and Mrs. Francis E. Hanlon.

Miss Rosemary Flynn, Miss Mary Collins, Miss Carol Persons and Mrs. Jerome B. Maggee are contacting junior members of the parish and will also assist at the tea table.

Service Unit To Give Show For Children

Republican Club Officers Named

The Republican Business and Professional Women's Club will have a dinner meeting at 6

The people of St. Mark were quick to welcome and celebrate the priest who quickly went from Fr. Burke to Msgr. Burke to Bishop Burke, all while living in the St. Mark rectory as the pastor.

Rosary, Altar Society Tea Principals

Mrs. Frank D. Cooley, left, is the retiring president of the Rosary and Altar Society of St. Mark's Church, which is holding its membership tea and installation of new officers from 4.30 until 6.30 p. m. Sunday in the school auditorium, Woodward Ave. Mrs. Garrett P. Barton, center, is the new president of the organization, and Mrs. Joseph E. McElroy is chairman of the tea.

Church Group Will Sponsor Tea Sunday

Rosary, Altar Society Selects Committees

Mrs. Joseph E. McElroy is general chairman of the membership tea which the Rosary and Altar Society of St. Mark's Church will sponsor from 4.30 to 6.30 p. m. Sunday at the school auditorium in Woodward Ave.

Receiving guests will be the Most Rev. Joseph A. Burke, administrator of Buffalo diocese, Mrs. Fred D. Cooley, Mrs. Garrett P. Barton, Miss Inez Krauss, Mrs. George A. Hellerer and Mrs. John Clark.

The membership committee in charge of the affair includes Mrs. David F. Devine, Mrs. Thomas J. McCann, Mrs. Henry Harris and Mrs. Sheldon W. Leibold. Decorations will be supervised by Mrs. James N. Connelly and Mrs. Arthur J. McDonell.

Presiding at the urns will be Mrs. Anna Smith, Mrs. Cornelius J. O'Keefe, Miss Kathryn Moynihan, Miss Jane Moynihan, Mrs. John J. Boland, Mrs. Edward R. Emig and Mrs. Edward I. May.

The refreshments committee includes Mrs. Frank A. Kraft, Mrs. William E. Maloney, Mrs. T. J. Masterson, Mrs. J. A. Maxwell, Mrs. Joseph White, Mrs. Eleanor Darling, Mrs. Mary McDonough, Mrs. Charles A. Steffan, Mrs. Edward V. Oakley and Miss Lucy Feldt. Publicity is being handled by Mrs. John P. Saxer.

Newly-elected officers who will be installed at the tea are Mrs. Barton, president; Mrs. Clark, vice-president; Mrs. Devine, secretary, and Mrs. McCann, treasurer. Miss Patricia O'Brien will be the soloist, accompanied by Mrs. Rogers Curtin.

Kenmore GOP To Celebrate

The 11th annual birthday dinner of the Kenmore Republican Women's Organization will be held at 6.30 p. m. next Thursday, in the parish hall of Kenmore Methodist Church, Landers Rd., Kenmore.

Home Nursing Class Planned

A class in the new streamlined Red Cross Home Nursing course will begin on Monday, October 23d and will meet on Monday, Wednesday and Friday from 2 to 4 p. m. for two weeks only, in the Chapter

The Rosary Society, Altar Society, and The St. Mark Guild all held special teas in honor of Bishop Burke's arrival and elevation.

His Parish Answers Plea of Red Cross

MSGR. JOSEPH A. BURKE

170 Members Of St. Mark's To Give Blood

Will Meet at School Friday for Donations

In response to the plea of the Buffalo Chapter of the American Red Cross for blood donations, 170 parishioners of St. Mark's Church, Woodward Avenue and Amherst Street, are expected to come to the school auditorium next Friday between 3 and 7.30 p. m. to give a pint of blood each to the Red Cross for conversion into blood plasma for America's fighting forces.

Msgr. Joseph A. Burke, pastor, and Thomas V. Ray, chairman of the committee, arranged for the special visit of the Red Cross Blood Bank to the church.

"This activity is a highly patriotic movement and the turnout is likely to exceed our original expectations," Ray said last night. "In the rear of St. Mark's Church is displayed an honor roll with the names of members now serving in our armed forces. It is a most impressive list.

"Now the members of St. Mark's will have the opportunity to honor those who left for the various war fronts by responding to the Red Cross call for donations of blood. All members of the parish have been invited to contribute.

"We are enlisting this parish blood-donor group in an effort to save the lives of our fighting sons on the battlefields. Blood is needed and needed badly for all the boys serving their country and our country throughout the world."

Msgr. Burke has arranged to station Boy and Girl Scouts in front of the church at all masses today to accept offers. The Scouts will be augmented by a special committee of women directed by Mrs. George J. Goetz.

As a veteran of The First World War, Bishop Burke made sure the people of St. Mark did their part in the war effort during World War II.

Seal Bishop Duffy's Secret Records

The record of the late Most Rev. John A. Duffy's bishopric was officially closed today when the Most Rev. Joseph A. Burke, administrator of the Buffalo Diocese, sealed with adhesive tape the secret archives of the diocese in the Chancery vaults at 50 Franklin St. The seals, affixed in the presence of the Rt. Rev. John J. Nash, V. G., P. A., vicar general of the diocese, will remain until removed by the successor to Bishop Duffy.

As Buffalo's Auxiliary Bishop, Bishop Burke tended to many duties and affairs outside of the parish. In 1944, he acted as Administrator of the Diocese after the death of Bishop Duffy (above, *Buffalo Evening News* photo.)

Left: Bishop Burke (right) poses with one of TV's earliest stars, Bishop Fulton Sheen. (*Courier-Express photo*)

A Buffalo Scrapbook: St. Mark's Roman Catholic Parish

The Most Rev. Joseph A. Burke, V.G., D.D.
Pastor of St. Mark's

Bishop Burke, From a 1948 play program

The Loving Legacy of Fr. Braun and Sr. Jeanne

St. Mark in the 1940's

Above: The church, 1948. Below: Bishop Burke stands among the eighth grade graduates of St. Mark School on the steps of the church.

A Buffalo Scrapbook: St. Mark's Roman Catholic Parish

Youthful Philanthropist Aids Toy Shop's Work

Six-year-old Jackie Fleet, Jr., of 60 Russell Avenue, a second grade pupil at St. Mark's School, decided a while ago that he'd aid Buffalo's needy boys and girls by saving his pennies and contributing them to The Courier-Express Christmas Toy Fund. Jackie accumulated $1 and made a personal presentation to Miss Virginia Graham at the Toy Shop yesterday. Acknowledgment of money contributions will appear regularly until Christmas in The Courier-Express.

Buffalo Courier Express, 1939

Buffalo Courier-Express, 1954

Sister Maria Stella, Sister of St. Joseph.

Principal of St. Mark School, 1954-57

A Buffalo Scrapbook: St. Mark's Roman Catholic Parish

Msgr. Eugene A. Loftus

St. Mark Pastor 1953-70

It took Bishop Burke nearly a year to name his successor. Bishop Burke installed The Right Rev. Eugene A. Loftus as St. Mark's pastor on February 15, 1953.

Niagara Falls Gazette

Born in 1898, Msgr. Loftus was ordained in 1924, and served in several parishes until he was named the Director of Catholic Charities in 1939, a role he'd continue as St. Mark's pastor.

Over his 30 years at the helm, from 1939 until his retirement in 1970, Catholic Charities raised over $63 million.

Children in Parkside remember Msgr. Loftus' big black car driving slowly through the streets of the neighborhood from the downtown Catholic Charities offices to the parish. Some even remember Monsignor's cigar sticking ever so slightly out the rear window as ashes were flicked.

As one of the most well-known and powerful priests of the diocese, Msgr. Loftus received many awards and honors during his lifetime and his 17 years at St. Mark. Perhaps most indicative of the level of respect for Msgr Loftus comes from a 1974 joint resolution from Buffalo Mayor Stanley Makowski and the Buffalo Common Council, naming the intersection of Washington and Genesee Streets as "Monsignor Loftus Plaza."

A Buffalo Scrapbook: St. Mark's Roman Catholic Parish

Right to Pick Own Charity Agency Cited

There is nothing in the philosophy of America that holds a religious agency equipped to serve the community should be confined for fear the State might recognize the church, the director of the annual Catholic Charity Appeal said yesterday.

The Rt. Rev. Eugene A. Loftus, pastor of St. Mark's Church, addressed the sixth Lenten Bellarmine Conference in Christ the King Chapel, Canisius College. Msgr. Loftus said there is nothing in American philosophy that mandates keeping private agencies out once a case has been referred to a public agency.

He declared the private agency still has a charter, aim and ambition to serve, and pointed out that persons in America are free to choose their own charitable agency and insist upon going to the hospital or clinic of their own choice.

"If we have approached the crossroads on this question then there is no reason why we should not express our concern and reenumerate our convictions," he said. "We have no desire to be critical of the hard-working staffs of public departments, but partnership is where we get things done with the least possible duplication and the least cost."

Msgr. Loftus said the Catholic Social Movement has a huge potential—the use of the volunteer. He said a good volunteer program can provide the "Minute Man" of our day, the good Samaritan on every road.

The Rev. Joseph F. Magner, assistant pastor of St. Mark's Church, celebrated Benediction of the Most Blessed Sacrament following the sermon. The conferences are sponsored annually in Lent by the college Alumni Association.

Msgr. Loftus was an in demand speaker around the Diocese, and is remembered as a firebrand in the St. Mark pulpit. A speech offered to graduates of St. Joseph Academy in Lockport reflect his style:

A few generations ago, we clung to the highest ideals. Today, instead of those ideals, the emphasis is on things of sense. A few generations ago, our family life was the object of our country, was the hope of our society, also a hope of womanhood in particular. Today, that is even being threatened and blighted at its very source. You are facing a world which would call you 'down from your tower' of tradition and this world would prefer to place the accent on the body rather than on the soul. It would prefer to accent time rather than eternity. It would prefer to accent success rather than sanctity; it would prefer to accent social prestige rather than simple sincerity. It would prefer to accent appearance rather than reality. It would prefer to accent man rather than God.

> **JOIN THIS MEMORABLE**
>
> ## MARIAN YEAR EVENT
>
> Religious Tour at Easter Time to the Holy Shrine of Our Lady of Guadalupe in Mexico. Under the Personal Leadership of the Right Reverend Monsignor Eugene A. Loftus.
>
> *Including:*
>
> **ALL EXPENSES — 9 DAY TOUR**
>
> Leaving April 15th, and Returning April 23rd
> $458.90 per Person — Double Room Basis
> $476.90 per Person — Single Room Basis
>
> *For Complete Details and Descriptive Literature...*
>
> **CALL—VI. 0401 or WA. 5540 or**
> **WRITE—RT. REV. MSGR. E. A. LOFTUS**
>
> St. Mark's Rectory
> 401 Woodward Ave., Buffalo 14, N. Y.

Msgr. Loftus' high profile extended to organizing pilgrimages to Mexican shrines, and having Mass from St. Mark televised live on Channel 4.

> # Radio-TV Highlights
>
> **A.M.**
> **11:00—Ch. 4—C H U R C H — High** Mass from St. Mark's Church, Buffalo. Rt. Rev. Msgr. Eugene A. Loftus. Live. 60 min.
>
> **P.M.**
> **12:00—Ch. 7—CHALLENGE GOLF** —A repeat match pairs Gary

A Buffalo Scrapbook: St. Mark's Roman Catholic Parish

BUFFALO COURIER-EXPRESS
Sunday, Nov. 7, 1954   29-A

Bishop to Lay Cornerstone At St. Mark's

The Most Rev. Joseph A. Burke, DD, bishop of Buffalo, will lay the cornerstone for St. Mark's School addition, 401 Woodward Ave., at 4 Thursday afternoon.

Bishop Burke, a former pastor of St. Mark's Church, will be assisted in the ceremony by the Rev. Edward J. Walker, pastor of St. Joseph's Church, Fredonia, and the Rev. James N. Connelly, assistant director of the Missionary Apostolate, Delevan.

The Rev. John R. Culbert, an assistant pastor at St. Mark's, will be master of ceremonies.

The Rt. Rev. Eugene A. Loftus, pastor of St. Mark's, said completion date for the addition is next Feb. 1. The building includes a gymnasium and four classrooms. It will be faced with Indiana limestone in conformity with other church buildings.

Solemn Benediction, celebrated by Bishop Burke and deacons Father Walker and Father Connelly, will be in St. Mark's Church. The Rev. Joseph F. Magner, an assistant pastor at St. Mark's, will be master of ceremonies at the benediction.

Bishop Burke will attend a reception in the school hall after the benediction, where he will renew acquaintances with former parishioners.

The Loving Legacy of Fr. Braun and Sr. Jeanne

In 1953, St. Mark church was completely redecorated and modernized, and plans were put in place to expand the school with the building of a gymnasium, and adding classrooms in the space which had been an auditorium on the main building's second floor. Above: Bishop Burke, under the watchful eye of Msgr. Loftus, lays the cornerstone for the school's new gym. Below: One of St. Mark's new classrooms.

A Buffalo Scrapbook: St. Mark's Roman Catholic Parish

St. Mark in the 1950s

Mr. & Mrs. Donald W. Arthur are married, above. Below, The Riester Family on the steps of St. Mark. Right: 1957 paperboy clean sweep.

CLEAN SWEEP — It's pracically an all-Courier-Express staff of officers in the graduating class at St. Mark's School, Amherst and Woodward. Three of the four are C-E newspaperboys and the other has a brother who delivers this newspaper. Graduation ceremonies will be held at 3 June 23 in St. Mark's Church.

Jerry Evarts

Michael Duffett of 458 Crescent Ave. was elected president by girls and boys in the school's two eighth grades. Kevin Denny of 140 Greenfield St. was chosen vice president and Richard Kolb of 317 Woodward Ave. received high vote for class treasurer.

Kathleen Brady of 251 Summit Ave. was elected secretary. Her brother, Thomas, is a C-E newspaperboy and occasionally on a bright Sunday morning Kathleen covers the route with Thomas.

A majority of youngsters who deliver newspapers are respected by adults they serve. Popular vote choices of graduating students at St. Mark's indicate newspaperboys also develop personalities which stamp them to young associates as outstanding.

A Buffalo Scrapbook: St. Mark's Roman Catholic Parish

St. Mark Kindergarten Class of 1957

League Champs, 1954

Diocesan Drama champions, with Msgr. Loftus and Fr. Magner

Eighth grade class photo with Msgr. Loftus

A Buffalo Scrapbook: St. Mark's Roman Catholic Parish

The Drama of Bernadette

This year has been observed by St. Mark's Church, at Woodward Ave. and Amherst St., as the 50th anniversary of its founding. It also is the centenary of the Shrine of Lourdes in France. Appropriately, the young people of St. Mark's as their part of the parish's celebration, have drawn on the story of Lourdes to present the moving drama, "The Song of Bernadette," Jean and Walter Kerr's dramatization of the Franz Werfel novel. It is to be presented tonight, and Monday and Tuesday evenings in St. Mark's Auditorium. The play has been directed by Mrs. Raymond C. Lenahan, and costumes were designed by Tore Amico, who formerly lived in Paris. Production manager is Mrs. Robert W. Ramsey, and Paul D. Welch is in charge of all stage and lighting effects. St. Mark's has the unique distinction of having had two bishops drawn from its pastorate. First pastor, the Rev. John J. McMahon, became the Bishop of Trenton, N. J. Its fourth pastor is now the present Bishop of Buffalo, the Most Rev. Joseph A. Burke, D.D. The Right Rev. Msgr. Eugene A. Loftus, P.A., is the present pastor of St. Mark's. These photos by Elizabeth Kahle illustrate the story of the play.

From the Buffalo Courier-Express, 1958

IN THE PLAY, "The Song of Bernadette," Bernadette Soubirous (Roberta Phillips) sees a vision of indescribable beauty — her Lady of the Grotto. Her sister Marie (Colleen O'Shea), center, and friend Jeanne Abadie (Mary Aversano) are frightened when they come upon Bernadette in a trance.

The Loving Legacy of Fr. Braun and Sr. Jeanne

CONCERNED that Lourdes may become the laughingstock of France because of the crowds following Bernadette daily to the Grotto, Mayor Lacade (William Logal), right, orders the girl examined by Dr. Dozous (Frank Kenny). The doctor's report that she is normal prompts Lacade to order her arrest by Jacomet (Peter Hassett), the chief of police.

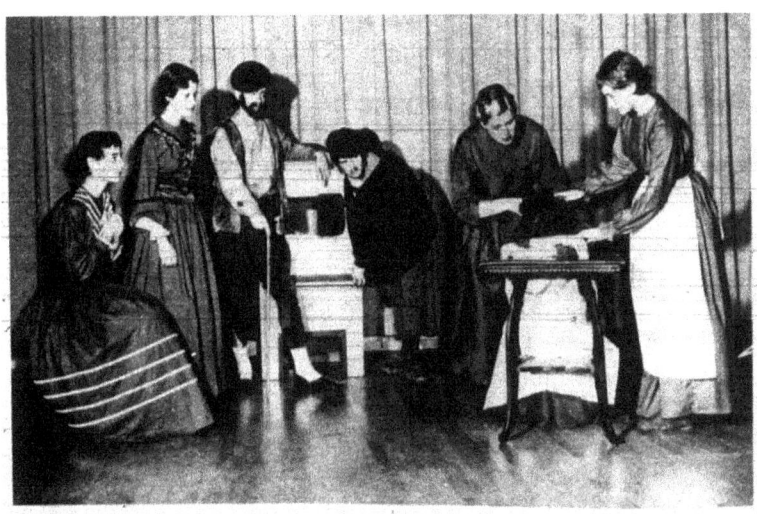

IN DIRE NEED, the Soubirous family lived in a house which had once been a prison. On the day of Bernadette's first vision, neighbors bring food and her father is offered a job. Left to right are Mary Littlefield, Frances Oldak, Paul Hartnett, Douglas MacLeod and Mrs. Paul B. Welch (Bernadette's father and mother), Roberta Phillips and Colleen O'Shea.

65

A Buffalo Scrapbook: St. Mark's Roman Catholic Parish

1958
The Golden Jubilee

ST. MARKS CHURCH

"Behold the Tabernacle of God with men"
APOCALYPSE XXI

TEXT OF BISHOP COLTON'S FIRST SERMON IN ST. MARKS—1908

The St. Mark community spent much of the late 50s through mid 60s celebrating the Golden Anniversaries of many milestones in the history of the parish, starting with the fiftieth anniversary of the founding of the parish in 1958.

The Loving Legacy of Fr. Braun and Sr. Jeanne

ST. MARK'S CHURCH
401 WOODWARD AVENUE
BUFFALO 14, NEW YORK

RT. REV. MSGR. EUGENE A. LOFTUS
PASTOR

January 24, 1958

To the Parishioners and Guests of St. Marks:

      All of us are one at Saint Marks, and one and all extend a very cordial greeting to you on the occasion of our First Golden Jubilee Social function. This dance at the Statler is a festive occasion, for we find joy in our affiliation with Saint Marks parish. We thank God in prayer for our fifty years of blessings. Among the blessings is the families and the people who compose Saint Marks. Get acquainted with them all! Don't miss one of them! The spirit of a church based on friendship counts very, very much. It brings happiness to the Jubilee and to the years ahead. Enjoy yourselves! May God bless you.

Eugene G. Loftus

A Buffalo Scrapbook: St. Mark's Roman Catholic Parish

OFFICERS OF ST. MARKS GUILD

Left to right: Miss Kathleen Hughes, *Secretary*; Mrs. William G. Bush, *Vice President*; Mrs. John P. Dwyer, *President*; Mrs. Fred E. Peters, *Secretary*; Mrs. Gerard R. Schumacher, *Treasurer*.

HOLY NAME SOCIETY—PAST PRESIDENTS

Front left to right: Dr. Zimmermann, Mr. Hoffmeyer, Fr. Magner, Mr. Wechter, Mr. Hassett.
Rear left to right: Mr. Kelly, Mr. Watt, Mr. Irwin, Mr. Espersen, Mr. Rittling, Mr. Helfter.

St. Mark Golden Jubilee booklet, 1958

Bishop to Offer Mass Sunday in St. Mark's Church

Parish He Directed For Decade Observing Its Golden Jubilee

The climax of events marking the Golden Jubilee year of St. Mark's parish will be reached on Sunday, April 27, with a solemn Pontifical Mass at 11 o'clock, to be celebrated by Most Rev. Joseph A. Burke, D.D., Bishop of Buffalo.

Most Rev. Leo R. Smith, D.D., Auxiliary Bishop of Buffalo, will be present in the sanctuary.

Deacons of honor to Bishop Burke, who will be returning to the parish he served as pastor from 1942 to 1952, will be Rev. Lawrence J. DiGiovanni and Rev. Harry W. Osborne.

Deacons of honor to Bishop Smith will be Very Rev. Philip E. Dobson, S.J., and Rev. Henry J. Cromey, O.M.I.

Others Assisting

Rt. Rev. Msgr. Francis Garvey will be archpriest. Deacon of the Mass will be Rev. Edward J. Walker, and subdeacon, Rev. John R. Culbert. Master of ceremonies will be Rev. Robert E. Murphy and Rev. Robert D. Duggan, assisted by Rev. Joseph F. Magner, Rev. James F. Chambers, Rev. James N. Connelly and Donald Trautman, a seminarian.

Rt. Rev. Msgr. Eugene A. Loftus is pastor of St. Mark's.

Music will be under the direction of John F. Gunderman, organist. Members of the Fourth Degree Knights of Columbus will form the color guard and the Holy Name Society the honor guard.

Concludes November 2

The next event in the jubilee observance, which opened with a solemn Midnight Mass on January 1, will be the school children's golden jubilee pageant in the auditorium on Friday, May 2, at 8:15 p.m. and Sunday, May 4, at 2:30 p.m.

On Sunday, June 22, at 1 p.m. the parish's golden jubilee shrine in honor of the Sacred Heart will be dedicated.

On All Souls Day, November 2, there will be a Memorial Communion Sunday for all deceased pastors, priests, religious and parishioners.

Buffalo Evening News

A Buffalo Scrapbook: St. Mark's Roman Catholic Parish

Bishop Takes Part in St. Mark's Golden Jubilee

Rt. Rev. Msgr. Eugene A. Loftus, pastor of St. Mark's Church, kisses the ring of Most Rev. Joseph A. Burke, D.D., as the Bishop enters the church for the Golden Jubilee Mass which he celebrated. During the Mass Bishop Burke announced that Msgr. Loftus had been made a Prothonotary Apostolic by His Holiness, Pope Pius XII. Bishop Burke, in his sermon, recalled the great work done by the priests and people of St. Mark's and told of the pleasant years he spent there as pastor until his elevation as Bishop of Buffalo. On Sunday, June 22, at 1 p.m., St. Mark's golden jubilee shrine in honor of the Sacred Heart will be dedicated. The jubilee will end with a Mass on All Souls Day, November 2, for deceased members of the parish.

from the Buffalo Diocesan newspaper

The Loving Legacy of Fr. Braun and Sr. Jeanne

One of the new classrooms added to St. Mark school in 1954.

From the St. Mark Golden Jubilee booklet, 1958

Sisters of St. Joseph maintaining the new school library

A Buffalo Scrapbook: St. Mark's Roman Catholic Parish

The Sisters of St. Joseph host a meeting of the Western New York Catholic Library Association at St. Mark

The Loving Legacy of Fr. Braun and Sr. Jeanne

Houses for Sale—Double

ST. MARK'S Parish, freshly painted exterior. Each flat has living room with woodburning fireplace, dining room, kitchen, 3 bedrooms; recreation room and bar in basement, $22,500. George Mills, W. H. Fitzpatrick, AT. 0210.

WEST OAKWOOD, 78, St. Mark's Parish, lower 2 bedroom apt. with 12x26 living room, modern kitchen and bath; (2) 1 bedroom apts. on second floor. Asking $17,500. Inspect Offers are always considered. Lunz Realty, PA. 4545.

During the era when your parish was strictly determined by where you lived, homes in St. Mark's Parish often demanded a premium.

room & 2nd kitchen. FA. 6946.

ST. MARK'S Parish, Woodward, charming 4-bedrooms, modern kitchen, 1½ baths, deep lot for the kiddies, garages, offers accepted. Munro Realtors, RI. 8605, for appt. only. PA. 1199.

TONAWANDA, your choice of new 3-bedroom Ranches, Cape Cods, split levels.

Act of Consecration

Heavenly Father, in the Name of Jesus Christ, I consecrate to thee all my activities during this coming week. My labors, my joys, my pleasures, my disappointments, which I offer through the Sacred Heart, to Thy Sovereign Majesty, in honor of the abiding presence of Jesus, in the Blessed Sacrament, and in thanksgiving for the many favors bestowed upon me. Amen.

Recited every Sunday in St. Marks by the Congregation.

From the St. Mark Golden Jubilee booklet, 1958

A Buffalo Scrapbook: St. Mark's Roman Catholic Parish

St. Mark's to Celebrate Anniversary of Church

St. Mark's Roman Catholic Church, which began in a small wooden chapel, will celebrate Sunday the 50th anniversary year of its present building at Amherst and Woodward.

Solemn Pontifical Mass at 10 in the morning will be celebrated by the Most Rev. James A. McNulty, bishop of the Diocese of Buffalo.

St. Mark's has 1,372 families today. It had only 32 when the Rev. John J. McMahon founded the parish in 1908. Soon the little wooden chapel, only 40 by 70 feet, was built at the present location. It had four Italian marble statues still used in the present church.

Fr. McMahon broke ground for today's stone church in 1914, and it opened the next year.

Served by Bishop Burke

A later pastor became bishop of Buffalo, the Most Rev. Joseph A. Burke, who served St. Mark's from 1942 until he became bishop in 1952. Ten years later Bishop Burke died in Rome.

The Rt. Rev. Eugene A. Loftus, director of appeals for Catholic Charities, has been pastor since 1953. He will be archpriest at the anniversary Mass.

Appropriately the 50th anniversary year of the church's building will be celebrated on the Feast of St. Mark.

Deacon of the Mass will be a former assistant pastor, the Rev. John R. Culbert of St. Vincent de Paul Church in Attica. The subdeacon will be another former assistant at St. Mark's, the Rev. Joseph F. Magner of St. Patrick's, Fillmore.

Others to Officiate

Deacons of honor will be the Rt. Rev. Msgr. Francis Garvey of St. Joseph's New Cathedral, a former assistant pastor of St. Mark's, and the Very Rev. Msgr. Maurice Woulfe of Infant of Prague Parish in Cheektowaga, a former resident member of St. Mark's staff.

Masters of ceremonies will be the Rev. Paul V. Durkin, assistant pastor of St. Mark's, and the Rev. William J. McDonnel, secretary to Bishop McNulty.

A reception will be held from 3 to 5 Sunday afternoon.

Seven years after celebrating the 50th anniversary of the parish, in 1965, St. Mark celebrated the 50th anniversary of the present church. Bishop Burke died in 1962, and was succeeded by Bishop James McNulty, who led the celebration of the Mass.

The Loving Legacy of Fr. Braun and Sr. Jeanne

St. Mark's Celebrates Golden Anniversary

The golden anniversary of St. Mark's Catholic Church, 401 Woodward Ave., was celebrated with the cutting of a cake and a reception in the church auditorium.

From left are: The Rt. Rev. Msgr. Eugene A. Loftus, the pastor; John W. Johnson, a St. Mark's altar boy in 1919-1921; Philip J. O'Shea, general chairman of the reception, who was born in 1909 on the present church site, and Mrs. Thomas Carey, 93, of 455 Crescent Ave., one of the church's oldest parishioners.

The Most Rev. James A. McNulty, bishop of Buffalo, celebrated a Solemn Pontifical Mass of Thanksgiving. Msgr. Loftus served as archpriest and past and present assistant pastors of St. Mark's assisted at the Mass. The event was held Sunday.

A Buffalo Scrapbook: St. Mark's Roman Catholic Parish

Family Finery Is Sewn by Mother of 8

By MARY RAHILL

A TRADITION—New spring clothes are as much a tradition of Easter Sunday as lilies, going to church and egg hunts. Children usually wear their new spring outfits for the first time on Easter Sunday and even Mom is inclined to save that new chapeau for the holiday.

Such is the case with the Howard V. Burke family of Summitt Ave. But instead of rushing about downtown searching for the right ensemble for each child, Mrs. Burke planned the outfits at home, bought the material "at a bargain" and made both the children's spring outfits and her own.

ELEGANT EIGHT—Today all eight of the Burke children are handsomely outfitted. Peter Aloysius, 9, and the twins, Paul Aloysius and Philip Aloysius, 5, are wearing Harris tweed jackets with gabardine trousers. Eight-year-old Mary Jeanne and Mary Josephine, 5, have print dresses with full skirts and velvet sashes.

The outfits worn by Robert Aloysius, 3½, and Joseph Aloysius, 2, combine red and white plaid jackets of tarpon cloth with navy blue, short pants. Even their broadcloth Eton shirts were made by Mom. Nor was 9-month-old Howard Vincent Aloysius forgotten. He has on a new shirt and trousers made of navy sailcloth.

BLACK CREPE—Fashioned of black wool crepe, Mrs. Burke's costume is styled with a blouson jacket and slim skirt and accented with black and white accessories.

Before early Mass this morning at St. Mark's Church the younger children discovered their Easter baskets, which had been carefully concealed by Peter and Mary Jeanne. The family will spend the day at home.

How does a busy mother with meals and household duties manage to make complete outfits for eight children? "I can do it because I love sewing and find it a means of relaxation," Mrs. Burke says. And she does have a woman help with the cleaning.

NOT OVERNIGHT—This talented mother "didn't make the costumes overnight." She has been working on them for several months.

"I'm a fast sewer, but it still took about two weeks for each of the boys' jackets," she said. Though she works fast, Mrs. Burke strives not to sacrifice detail and those finishing touches that are the mark of the expert. Mary Jeanne's dress for instance, is worn with a short, navy blue jacket that is lined with the print of the dress and trimmed with a white collar and pearl buttons.

CREATIVE—The project was made easier when Mrs. Burke found the Harris tweed suit-coat material in two- and three-yard lengths in a local store. She estimates that the jackets cost her about $5 each. "Jackets of the same quality are about $35 in a store," she explained.

One of the pleasures of her hobby, says Mrs. Burke is its creativeness. "I find mending horrible," she says, "but I find satisfaction in completing an outfit for one of the children."

QUALITY — Actually, Mrs. Burke is not s u r e how economical her hobby is because she counts the cost of her cleaning woman against her sewing expenses. She is able to use fine quality fabrics, though, whereas she might have to sacrifice quality in purchasing ready-made outfits.

Sewing takes time from reading and other hobbies Mrs. Burke would like to pursue, but she finds that she can sew with the children around. So it's a good hobby for a mother who must be home to care for young children.

MARINE VET — A native of Milwaukee, Wis., Mrs. Burke studied sewing in high school. She was studying business administration at Marquette University, Milwaukee, when she met her husband, a native Buffalonian. A few months later Howard Burke entered the Marines. They were married after World War II, following Mr. Burke's graduation from Fordham University in New York.

After Mr. Burke completed law studies at Notre Dame University, Notre Dame, Ind., they moved to Buffalo. He is the law partner of James L. Kane, president of the Buffalo Council, AFL-CIO.

BISHOP'S HONOR—Mr. Burke is the nephew of the late Most Rev. Joseph Aloysius Burke, bishop of the Buffalo Diocese. It was in honor of Bishop Burke and St. Aloysius, patron saint of youth, that Mr. and Mrs. Burke included the name Aloysius in their sons' names.

Marie Burke has taken on diverse responsibilities. She devotes 40 hours a year to the Junior Board of Kenmore Mercy Hospital. She and Mr. Burke have been active in the Christian Family Movement promoting Catholic ideals in marriage and family life.

EXCHANGE PLAN—Both are on the board of the Foundation for International Co-operation, a student exchange program under the auspices of the Bishop's Committee of the Buffalo Diocese. Two brothers from Quito, Ecuador, lived with the Burke family last year while attending Bishop Fallon High School.

In conjunction with the exchange program, Mrs. Burke studies Spanish one evening a week at D'Youville C o l l e g e. Spanish records are played during the evening meals to familiarize the children with the language.

DISCIPLINE — Mrs. Burke spends what time she can from her busy schedule promoting the work of the Le Leche League, an organization which advocates breast feeding of infants.

Discipline with love is the credo Mr. and Mrs. Burke use in rearing their children. "As a lawyer," says Mrs. Burke, "Howard sees so many of the problems people face who live their lives without discipline."

Buffalo Courier-Express, 1963

The Loving Legacy of Fr. Braun and Sr. Jeanne

Joseph Robert Mrs. Burke and Howard Paul Mary Jeanne Peter Mr. Burke
              Mary Josephine Philip
... the Burke family has a "dress rehearsal" for Easter Sunday

Mrs. Burke Peter Mary Jeanne Mary Josephine
The Burke children model Easter outfits.

A Buffalo Scrapbook: St. Mark's Roman Catholic Parish

Fashions Shown at St. Mark's

The St. Mark's Guild fashion show, "Fashion Vote '68," will be held Monday, Oct. 21, at 8:30 p.m. in Bishop's auditorium.

Mrs. Joseph J. DeFalco and Mrs. Edwin W. Helman will be co-chairmen of the event.

Committee heads are Mrs. Robert P. Hazelet, Mrs. James P. McLellan, Mrs. Verdun V. Vashinder, Mrs. Louis F. Scholl, Mrs. Dominic J. Liponi, Mrs. David J. Doran, Mrs. John F. Downing, Mrs. Thomas J. Murphy, Mrs. Thomas M. Myszkiewicz, Mrs. Joseph W. Pericak, Mrs. Vincent J. Lesh.

Also Mrs. Dominic J. Cipolla, Mrs. Francis P. Gaughn, Mrs. Philip L. Burger, Mrs. Harold Sundberg and Mrs. Louis J. Curto.

Mrs. Louis Curto   Mrs. Robert Hazelet   Mrs. Thomas Myszkiewicz

ST. MARK'S - 1968

St. Mark, 1968

Msgr. Loftus with Vice President Hubert Humphrey, 1967

A Buffalo Scrapbook: St. Mark's Roman Catholic Parish

SAINT MARK'S

VOLUME II • MARCH, 1968 • NO. 5   published by St. Mark's Holy Name Society

Rev. Mears to Speak

Lenten activities at St. Mark's will take an ecumenical turn when the Rev. John D. Mears of the Episcopal Church of the Good Shepherd speaks Tuesday, April 9, at 8:30 p.m. in the auditorium. Father Mears' address is sponsored by the Holy Name Society.

Ecumenical aspects of Christian life today will be Father Mears' chief topic. A dialogue with members of the audience will follow the talk.

The evening will conclude with a special Lenten scripture service and contemporary religious music.

Richard Griffin is chairman.

Lenten Services Listed

Mass will be celebrated Monday through Friday evenings during Lent at 7:30 p.m. Stations of the Cross will follow Friday evening mass. Other Lenten services will be held Friday afternoons at 12:45 and 2:30 for the school children and everyone else who finds it more convenient to attend afternoon services.

Guild's Baked Goods Sale Scheduled for March 24

St. Mark's Guild Baked Goods and Candy Sale will be held in the school Sunday, March 24, after the 8 a.m. mass until 12:30.

Every woman in the parish is asked to bring her contribution to the school cafeteria Saturday afternoon or Sunday morning, or to call Mrs. Thomas McLaughlin, 836-3439, or Mrs. John R. Eagan, 836-6139, for pick-up.

Co-chairmen Mrs. A. John Amico and Mrs. Eagan are busily working with the following committee:

Mrs. Robert G. Klein, baked goods; Mrs. Richard C. Hartley and Mrs. John R. Cole, candy; Mrs. Dominick J. Cipolla and Mrs. Vincent J. Lesh, basket of cheer; Mrs. Thomas J. Murphy, finance; Mrs. McLaughlin, pickup; Mrs. Russel M. Applegate, telephone; Mrs. P. B. Cotter, publicity; Mrs. Walter R. Gehl, ways and means; and Mrs. Thomas R. Lynett, honorary chairman.

Yeast goods and pies are preferred.

Automobile Polish Mfrs & Distrs

(J. S. McGarry, St. Mark's Parishioner)

BUY **Garry's** FAMOUS AUTOMOTIVE PRODUCTS AT ANY OF THESE NEIGHBORHOOD BUSINESSES:

Wally Gulf Linden and Colvin	Ken Gilbert Gulf 1274 Hertel	Ed Marquart Mobil Parkside and Hertel
Parkside Gulf 281 Parkside Ave.	Stan Boccolucci 1336 Hertel	Jesse Tronolone Atlantic Parkside and Hertel
Central Park Esso 1600 Amherst	Summit Hardware & Electric 1469 Hertel	Herb Hoegel Gulf Hertel and Starin
Hertel Hardware & Plumbing 1275 Hertel	Pirson-Layer 1473 Hertel	Turner & Clark Texaco 1871 Hertel
Wangler Hardware & Electric Main and Fillmore		Ed and Bob's Texaco 72 E. Amherst St.

Automobile Dealers

JIM ALLEN...836-1000

IS THE MAN TO SEE FOR A NEW BUICK, OPAL OR QUALITY USED CAR.

BARTLETT BUICK, INC. 3080 Main St.

Beauty Shops

Phone: 836-8975

The Golden Room Coiffures

309 Parkside Avenue — Opposite the Zoo

Cutting — Coloring — Permanents — Hair Styling — Wigs and Wiglets

Bowling

ALLIED BOWLING CENTER INC.

325 Manhattan Ave.

Buffalo 14, New York

836-4150

Cleaners & Dyers

TF 4-6892

ARTKRAFT TAILORS & CLEANERS

PLANT & OFFICE: 26 RODNEY AVENUE

BUFFALO, N.Y. 14214

JOHN PALMERI   DELIVERY SERVICE

PHONE 837-8410

DIAL CLEANERS AND SHIRT LAUNDRY, INC.

2496 MAIN ST.   BUFFALO, N.Y. 14214

April 28 Affair to Honor Members in Religious Life

Sunday, April 28, will be Religious Family Recognition Day at St. Mark's. Beginning at 2:30 p.m. in the auditorium, the parish will honor its members who are in or studying for the religious life.

High point of the afternoon will be a folk mass concelebrated by the visiting priests.

The program will include music by The Singing Nuns of the Mount St. Joseph Motherhouse and students from the Diocesan Preparatory Seminary.

Mr. and Mrs. Kenneth Barth, Mr. and Mrs. Edward Fallon, Sister Marie, S.S.J., and Rev. Albert W. Clody are chairmen of the celebration, which is a direct result of the religious life census recently conducted in the parish.

Tickets Sold to 151

One hundred and fifty-one couples purchased tickets to the Holy Name Society's Hippie Hop held in the auditorium on February 23.

A Buffalo Scrapbook: St. Mark's Roman Catholic Parish

Funeral Directors

LUX & SONS . . . *Funeral Home*
2528 Main St. — Joseph F. Lux, Mgr.
TF 3-6227
Lady Attendant
75 YEARS OF RELIABLE SERVICE

McKENDRY-DENGLER FUNERAL HOME INC.
2540 MAIN STREET   833-1202

"This historic house, built in 1840, now restored and remodeled lends itself most graciously for use as a funeral home."

TF 2-2123   TT 4-0523
GEORGE J. ROBERTS & SONS
Funeral Home
Private Off-Street Parking — Centrally Air Conditioned
2400 MAIN STREET   205 LINWOOD AVENUE

TRAPP
FUNERAL HOME

Blood Total Tops 100 Pints On Way to 260-Pint Goal

With donations received at the Red Cross Blood Center on Delaware Avenue, St. Mark's Blood Bank has now been credited with 108 pints toward its 260-pint quota. Before June 1, 152 more pints must be donated if every parishioner and his family is to remain covered. On Thursday, May 2, the Bloodmobile will visit St. Mark's for the last time this program year. In the meantime, donations may be made at 786 Delaware Avenue by phoning 886-7500 for an appointment.

KASTING-McGINNIS FUNERAL HOME
833-4219

2268 Main St.   Buffalo, N.Y.

KENNETH M. KELLY
Funeral Home
2554 MAIN ST.
883-3323   PARKING

ST. MARK'S NEWS
Chairman -- Paul V. Offermann, 836-2044 (home).
Editor -- Donald W. Boyd Jr., 874-1497 (office), 836-3993 (home).
Advertising Mgr. -- David J. Hickey, 836-1496 (home).

3

Father Madsen Surveys Attitudes Toward Parents

Attitudes of pre-teenage children and their parents toward each other are the subject of a study being conducted by Rev. John W. Madsen.

Father Madsen has received some unexpectedly profound responses to three simple questions he has asked of seventh and eighth graders at St. Mark's School, and he hopes to relate these answers to those of the parents.

Participants in the survey are asked to:

1. List three things you don't like about your parents;
2. State what serious subject, if any, you have ever discussed with your parents;
3. Sum up in one sentence your parents' good qualities.

Fur Business–Retail

CALL 833-8853
FURS BY
SARAH CLARK
2290 MAIN ST.   BUFFALO, N.Y. 14214

Hardware–Retail

WANGLER'S
Electric & Hardware
for Every Need

MAIN & FILLMORE   OPEN THUR. & FRI. till 9

Insurance

CLAUSS AND COMPANY
INSURANCE

TELEPHONE
886-6600

CHARLES J. CLAUSS

735 DELAWARE AVENUE ✶ BUFFALO, NEW YORK 14209

Interior Decorators' & Designers

Peggy Keenan Reed Interiors
Thomas and Peggy Reed
COMPLETE INTERIOR
DECORATING SERVICE
2661 MAIN ST.   TF 4-1712

Lawn Mowers

BUFFALO LAWN MOWER SUPPLIES
2324 MAIN STREET
836-2356
Repairs - Sales - Parts
Engines - Lawn Mowers - Snow Blowers

Annual Father-Son Affair Coming on Friday, May 17

The Father-Son mass and communion sponsored by the Holy Name Society will take place Sunday, May 17. Mass will be at 5:30, followed by a fish dinner in the cafeteria at 6:30.

Richard Wylegala, chairman, has named Arthur Chambers and James Connors to assist him in planning the event.

St. Mark's Guild to Pick Five Directors, April 22

St. Mark's Guild will elect five new members to its 15-member board of directors at the regular Guild meeting on Monday, April 22.

Nominated to serve three-year terms are:

Marcy Amico (Mrs. A. John), 430 Crescent Avenue;

Winifred Boyd (Mrs. Donald W. Jr.), 541 Crescent Avenue;

Mamie Cipolla (Mrs. Dominick J.), 315 Woodward Avenue;

Ellen Grunthaner (Mrs. Robert L.), 98 Wallace Avenue;

Irene Klein (Mrs. Robert G.), 1467 Amherst Street;

Rosemary McMahon (Mrs. John J.), 100 Beard Avenue;

Nancy O'Dea (Mrs. William J. Jr.), 138 Depew Avenue;

Eleanor O'Mara (Mrs. Edward J.), 1702 Amherst Street;

Gloria Palmer (Mrs. George), 438 Woodward Avenue; and

Mary Ellen Schumacher (Mrs. Gerald A.), 206 Summit Avenue.

The new board will elect officers for next year early in May, and both newly-elected officers and board members will be installed May 20.

Candidates for the board were nominated by a committee headed by Mrs. Joseph J. DeFalco. Nominating committee members are

(continued on page 6)

Liquor Stores

ART DESMOND LIQUOR STORE
285 PARKSIDE AVE. (opposite Zoo)
Chilled Wines Ready To Serve
PARKING SPACE   836-1400

CONNELLY'S LIQUORS
2302 Main at West Oakwood
PHONE: 883-0068

Paint–Retail

McDB
McDOUGALL-BUTLER PAINTS
Finest Finishes for
School — Home — Industry

Pharmacists

DWYER'S PHARMACY
ROCCO BALLACCHINO, PROP.
2248 Main St. corner Florence
Buffalo, New York
Telephone: 834-1649
WE ACCEPT MEDICAID PRESCRIPTIONS

MAIN-FILLMORE PHARMACY
(Formerly Mayo-Smith)
2620 MAIN corner VERNON
DRIVE-IN   834-8888   FAST, FREE
OR PHONE   DELIVERY
Stop in and say hello to Erv and Ron

SMITHER & HILL DRUG CO., Inc.   2339 Main St
Phone 833-1111   Corner Le Roy
                                      Buffalo, N.Y

SMITHER'S
RELIABLE PHARMACIES
"If it's a prescription take it to Smither's"

ZIMDAHL'S PHARMACY, Inc.
2686 Main Street
(Corner of Amherst)
FREE DELIVERY — UTILITIES — MIDLAND CHARGE
Telephone 833-0039

Mass to Be Televised

The Annual Catholic Charities Mass will be televised from St. Mark's by WBEN-TV, Channel 4, Sunday, March 24, at 11 a.m. Rt. Rev. Msgr. Eugene A. Loftus, P.A., pastor of St. Mark's and director of the diocesan appeal, will preach. Rev. Robert J. Williamson will be celebrant, and Rev. Albert W. Clody and Rev. John W. Madsen will present the scriptural readings.

Other mass March 24 will be at 7, 8, 9, 10, 12:30, and 5.

Gym Open to Young Men

St. Mark's gymnasium is being used by 30 to 40 young adults on Monday, Tuesday, Wednesday, and Saturday nights from 7 to 10 in a supervised program sponsored by the Holy Name Society.

Directors...
(continued from page 5)

Mrs. Verdun V. Vasbinder, Mrs. Clifford Bonn, Mrs. Ernest Hanover, and Mrs. James Greco.

The five board members who will complete three-year terms this year are Mrs. Paul B. Cotter, Mrs. DeFalco, Mrs. Thomas R. Lynett, Mrs. Albert Riester Jr., and Mrs. Louis F. Scholl.

Blood Donor Limit Increased to 5

Effective Nov. 15, the Red Cross increased to five from four the number of times a person may give blood in one year. The increase followed the amending of a New York State Department of Health ruling that had restricted blood donations to four per year.

Photographic Equipment & Supplies– Retail

Masons BUFFALO PHOTO MATERIAL CO.
All Types of Amateur and Professional Supplies and Equipment
Audio-Visual Supplies, Sales, and Rentals.

37 NIAGARA STREET   BUFFALO, N.Y. 14202
JACK HOYT, Prop.   854-6305   *63 Years of Service*

Pizza

AVENUE PIZZA & SUBMARINE
Featuring Home-Made Sausage & Rolls

Fast Take-Out Service
Charles "Lou" Cortese
2612 MAIN STREET   1341 HERTEL AVENUE
837-4066   877-5959

Real Estate

HELEN L. LIPS REALTY, INC.
REAL ESTATE–INSURANCE
836-5151

Real Estate

W. H. FITZPATRICK & SONS, INC.
REAL ESTATE INSURANCE

JOHN H. KUHLMANN, *Vice President*   836-0210

Sacraments to Be Topic

Mothers of young children will exchange ideas on "Building the Child's Knowledge of the Sacraments" at meetings of the Bishop's Committee for Christian Home and Family discussion groups during April.

The groups will meet as follows:

Group I -- April 2, Grace McDonald, hostess, 60 Wellington Road, 833-4862.

Group II -- April 2, Pat Kuczkowski, hostess, 372 Crescent Avenue, 837-7780.

Group III -- April 2, Carol Ciracuse, hostess, 374 Woodward Avenue, 836-4285

Group IV -- April 3, Serena Pignatoro, hostess, 51 Greenfield Street, 834-0034.

Counsel in Confessions

The Sacrament of Penance is becoming more meaningful to students in St. Mark's School this Lent with "counseling" confessions. Father Clody and Father Madsen are providing the children an opportunity to talk out their problems with a priest during confession, with or without the confessional screen between them. This approach to Penance is one way of emphasizing that every sacrament is a personal encounter with Christ.

Rubbish Removal

DOWNING CONTAINER SERVICE
191 GANSON STREET
853-6117

Shopping Centers

Compliments of
The Merchants of Central Park Plaza
and
Assemblyman
Al. Hausbeck

Sporting Goods—Retail

HARTNETT'S
FOR ALL YOUR SPORTS NEEDS
1565 Hertel   833-9115

Telephone Answering Service

853-6650
McCALL TELEPHONE ANSWERING SERVICE
305 WALBRIDGE BLDG.   BUFFALO, N.Y. 14203

Wood Work

E. M. HAGER & SONS CO.
CUSTOM BUILT WOODWORK
MANUFACTURED, FINISHED, INSTALLED
WALTER L. HOFFMEYER, Pres.

The Loving Legacy of Fr. Braun and Sr. Jeanne

return requested
St. Mark's Holy Name Society; 401 Woodward Ave., Buffalo, N.Y. 14214

Non-Profit Organization
U. S. POSTAGE
P A I D
Permit No. 2478
Buffalo, N Y

Thomas Mysakiewicz
367 Woodward Ave.
Buffalo, N.Y. 14214

What's Going on At St. Mark's

MARCH 24, SUNDAY
Baked Goods and Candy Sale sponsored by St. Mark's Guild; Cafeteria; 8:45-12:30.

APRIL 5, FRIDAY
School closes for spring vacation.

APRIL 9, TUESDAY
Lenten activity for all parishioners sponsored by the Holy Name Society; talk by Rev. John D. Mears with scripture service and contemporary religious music; Auditorium; 8:30 p.m.

APRIL 22, MONDAY
St. Mark's Guild meeting; election of directors and speaker on St. Mark's Blood Bank; Cafeteria; 8:30 p.m.

APRIL 22, MONDAY
Holy Name Society District Three meeting; St. Mark's, host.

APRIL 22, MONDAY
School opens after spring vacation.

APRIL 28, SUNDAY
Religious Family Recognition Day; Auditorium; 2:30 p.m.

MAY 2, THURSDAY
St Mark's Blood Bank; spring visit of Red Cross Bloodmobile; Cafeteria.

MAY 5, SUNDAY
Corporate Communion Breakfast; St. Mark's Guild.

MAY 17, FRIDAY
Father-Son Mass and Corporate Communion sponsored by the Holy Name Society; mass in church at 5:30; fish fry in Cafeteria at 6:30 p.m.

MAY 20, MONDAY
St. Mark's Guild meeting; installation of officers; Cafeteria; 8:30 p.m.

St. Mark Holy Name Newsletter, mailed to parishioners, 1968

After 17 years at St. Mark, at the age of 72, Msgr. Loftus retired from the active priesthood. Vice Chancellor and diocesan architect Msgr. William Grant was named pastor of St. Mark, and also took over Msgr. Loftus' job as the Director of the Catholic Charities Appeal.

> Other changes included the retirement of Msgr. Eugene A. Loftus, P.A., director of the Catholic Charities Appeal since 1939 and pastor of St. Mark's Church for 17 years.
>
> Msgr. William J. Grant, vice chancellor of the diocese, will retain Msgr. Loftus' office, and also become the new pastor of St. Mark's Church on June 13.

Msgr. Grant attended Holy Family parish in South Buffalo, and was ordained in 1941.

At the outbreak of World War II, Fr. Grant enlisted in the Navy, and served as a chaplain throughout the war. Once stateside, he was active as the chaplain for the American Legion for decades.

St. Mark was a "bingo hold-out" for decades, but during Msgr. Grant's five year tenure as pastor, bingo was instituted to help ease financial burdens for the parish and the school.

Msgr. Grant left St. Mark in 1975. He also left the priesthood. He eventually married a fellow retired military colonel and VA nurse. Without children, William and Mary Grant left their estate to the Diocese of Buffalo.

The William J. Grant Trust was "established to provide for the health care needs of priests and seminarians and the training of nursing students."

The Rev. William J. Grant, 28, son of Mr. and Mrs. George E. Grant, 85 East Amherst St., has been commissioned a lieutenant, junior grade, in the Chaplains Corps and transferred to the Naval Air Station at Miami Beach, Fla. Formerly stationed at St. Columba's Church, Eagle and Hickory. Lieut. Grant entered service last January and was graduated from the William & Mary College, Va.

The Buffalo priest attended Holy Family School and the Little Seminary and was graduated from St. Bonaventure. He was ordained in June, 1941, by the Most Rev. John A. Duffy, bishop of Buffalo.

Rev. W. J. Grant

A Buffalo Scrapbook: St. Mark's Roman Catholic Parish

St. Mark in the 1970s

The Loving Legacy of Fr. Braun and Sr. Jeanne

St. Mark's Eighth Grade Class of 1972

BAD WEATHER...and time off from school, pushed Catholic Schools Week activities back at St. Mark's, 401 Woodward Ave. The students prepared a serious of skits and activities dramatizing their daily activities and achievements in school. A Greenich Village Cafe was only one of many projects put on by the students last Thursday night.

A Buffalo Scrapbook: St. Mark's Roman Catholic Parish

First Communion at St. Mark's, 1980, with Fr. Ochs presiding

Rev. Robert G. Ochs spent five years as pastor at St. Mark, from 1975 to 1980. He (and Msgr. Braun) were among 33 priests ordained by Bishop Burke at St. Joseph's New Cathedral on Delaware Avenue in 1954.

Fr. Ochs grew up in Kenmore, and spent many years after his ordination as an assistant pastor at St. Amelia's in Tonawanda, where he spent many years as the youth director.

While at St. Mark, he continued his work with children and furthered Vatican II directives to modernize the appearance of the church, including removal of the altar rails from the main altar. Fr. Ochs also renovated the rectory and encouraged the establishment of the school's Home School Association.

Fr. Ochs moved on from St. Mark to Blessed Sacrament Church in the Town of Tonawanda, where he died in 1984.

The Loving Legacy of Fr. Braun and Sr. Jeanne

TALKING IT OVER: The Rev. Robert G. Ochs, center, youth director at St. Amelia's Church, discusses the formation of a Catholic Youth Council with, from left, John Henderson, Judy Drum, Judy Henderson and Richard Nitto. Fr. Ochs has extended an invitation to all young people of the parish to attend a meeting in the school hall Thursday.

*Fr. Ochs spent most of his priesthood serving parishes in Tonawanda.
(Tonawanda News photos)*

HAPPY ANNIVERSARY, DEAR FATHER: The Rev. Robert G. Ochs was not quite "floored," but had to sit down when Grades 1 through 6 at St. Amelia's School wished him a "Happy Anniversary" at a surprise party in his honor Friday. The occasion marked the 10th anniversary of his ordination. He knew only that he and two other priests associated with St. Amelia's, the Rev. Paul Belzer and the Rev. Philip Badame, were to be honored at a reception Sunday by the church's Holy Name Society, Guild and Ladies of Charity. The "little old lady" presenting him with a gaily-wrapped gift is Karen Sroka. Others in the picture are, from left: Margaret Norton, the Rt. Rev. John L. McHugh, St. Amelia's senior pastor, the Rev. John Kelly, like the "anniversary boy," an assistant pastor for nine of those 10 years, and Catherine Gauthia.

A Buffalo Scrapbook: St. Mark's Roman Catholic Parish

Msgr. Francis Braun and Sr. Jeanne Eberle, 2009 *(WNY Catholic Weekly photo)*

The Loving Legacy of Fr. Braun and Sr. Jeanne

The Msgr. Braun/Sr. Jeanne Era

Sr. Jeanne Eberle came to St. Mark as principal in 1977. Three years later, Fr. Francis Braun came to St. Mark as pastor. For three decades, Father and Sister made St. Mark a warm, inviting community.

We've seen their love for us manifest in countless ways. Sister is always quick to offer a hug and a First Communion present. Father is there with a handshake or a high five, and a pizza party for the kids, with maybe a bottomless keg for their parents.

St. Mark was beaming with pride when Fr. Braun and Sr. Jeanne were chosen to receive the Bishop's Medal at the Catholic Education Dinner in 2009.

It was the perfect representation of who and what our beloved pair are and have meant to St. Mark.

First and foremost, their focus has been on our children and making sure they receive not only the best, but plenty of love and support along the way.

The awards were separate, but inexorably entwined and wholly dependent on one another—in much the same way each ran the church and the school.

The stories written about Sr. Jeanne and Fr. Braun for the "Making A Difference Dinner" program are a great place to start thinking about each of these amazing people as we celebrate their lives as a part of our lives.

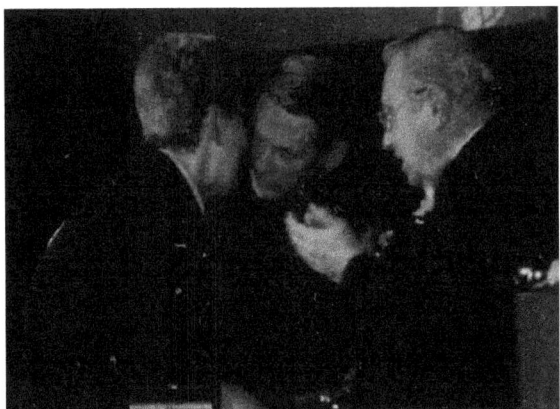

Bishop Kmiec looks on as Sister Jeanne and Msgr. Braun embrace as they receive The Bishop's Medal for their in promoting Catholic education.

A Buffalo Scrapbook: St. Mark's Roman Catholic Parish

From the Making a Difference Dinner 2009 program

Rev. Msgr. Francis Braun: Bishop's Medal Recipient

Each day at 7:40am, Msgr. Francis Braun stands at the doors of St. Mark School in North Buffalo and welcomes his young pupils to a new day of learning. Much like a shepherd watches his flock, Msgr. Braun stands guard to make sure nothing hinders the children's pathway. In his own words, "We aren't just providing knowledge; we are providing a safe environment, spiritually and physically. I watch to make sure this runs true."

During the course of his current tenure as pastor, Msgr. Braun has made the growth of St. Mark school one of his top priorities. The high standards of education that Msgr. Braun has successfully implemented at St. Mark are confirmed yearly by the recruitment of his students to top Buffalo Catholic high schools.

"My life, my calling is fulfilled when I see the children I have known since they were so little, grow up and appreciate their life. When they appreciate what they have to go through, what they did to get to that point that they are at know, then I know that I have made a difference in their lives," said Msgr. Braun. "Our school, our parish is like the glue that holds our community in Buffalo together. We all help each other, we all live for each other. In this way, our community and school is a family."

It has been this desire to maintain a faith-based, tight-knit community similar to that which he knew as a child that has kept Msgr. Braun at his post of pastor at St. Mark for almost thirty years.

Growing up in the St. James parish in the Bailey-Kensington area of Buffalo, Msgr. Braun remembers the positive impact that the parish priests had. As a result of this influence and his desire to make a difference, Msgr. Braun answered his calling to the priesthood. After graduating from Canisius High School, he entered Christ the King Seminary at St. Bonaventure University in Olean, NY and was ordained in 1954.

The Loving Legacy of Fr. Braun and Sr. Jeanne

One of his first assignments was teaching summer school in the Southern Tier. As he spent his days teaching religion to his young pupils, he began to see the true value of a Catholic education and the benefits that a Catholic school brings to a community.

Msgr. Braun continued to mold the young minds of Buffalo when he took a position at Bishop Turner High School located on the city's East Side. For the next 17 years, as he educated his students in Religious and English studies, Msgr. Braun also instilled Catholic values and morals within his young charges.

Even as his love of teaching grew, Msgr. Braun realized that his vocational calling was leading him back into pastoral life. His desire to remain in the city and to find a parish with a school led him to St. Mark. In 1980, Msgr. Braun was appointed pastor and as a result, both church and school have flourished and prospered.

Msgr. Braun shows the crowd the medal just awarded him by Bishop Kmiec.

A Buffalo Scrapbook: St. Mark's Roman Catholic Parish

From the Making a Difference Dinner 2009 program

Sr. Jeanne Eberle: Bishop's Medal Recipient

"If I can touch the life of one child, then I know my life has been a success" is the philosophy of Sister Jeanne Eberle, SSJ, principal of St. Mark School in Buffalo. "Obviously," chuckles Sister Jeanne, "I want it influence many, many children but knowing that I made a difference to one is enough for me."

It is this kind of caring that has kept Sister Jeanne at her post as principal of St. Mark School for the past thirty-two years. And it is this type of caring that has given her the strength to continually strive to help each and every child that has come through the doors of St. Mark. Each day, as she scrambles for time to complete all the necessary work to keep her school running, it is the thought of the children that she is influencing that keeps her ready for the next challenge that will undoubtedly come her way.

The responsibilities that Sister Jeanne faces as a Catholic school principal are vastly greater than administrative duties. Her understanding that her obligation is to not only provide a stellar academic setting, but surroundings where children are provided for spiritually, physically, emotionally, morally, and socially is what has made her tenure at St. Mark so successful. By reaching out to her students on their own level, Sister Jeanne has achieved a close relationship with her young charges and continually works to improve their quality of life, both at school and beyond.

Under her watchful eye, St. Mark has flourished into a prestigious academic institute within the Diocese of Buffalo. The majority of St. Mark students go on to Catholic high schools, and a large number of their students are recruited by prominent schools within the area. Sister Jeanne has witnessed first hand the effect that she has had on shaping the young minds that have walked her school halls.

With the help of the St. Mark Home School Association that she created, Sister Jeanne has turned the school into an athletic pillar within the community as well. Understanding that children need more in their lives than just scholastic resources, Sister Jeanne has created new after school and sports programs to help mold the entire character of the young children of St. Mark.

The latest addition to her athletic program, the St. Mark hockey team, rewarded Sister Jeanne for all of her hard work by having a perfect season so far.

The second oldest of ten children, Sister Jeanne received her Bachelor's in education from D'Youville and her Master's in education from Mount St. Joseph Teachers College. Sr. Jeanne also received a Doctorate from the State University of New York at Buffalo in Elementary Remedial Education.

Before she was appointed principal at St. Mark, Sister Jeanne taught at various elementary schools within the Diocese. She served as Assistant Professor and Director of Education and Graduate Divisions at Medaille College for nine years. Sister Jeanne has received the Religious Educator of the Year award and was honored with the Unsung Hero Award by the West Side Rowing Club in 2007.

Sister Jeanne Eberle accepts her Bishop's Medal Award as Bishop Kmiec looks on.

A Buffalo Scrapbook: St. Mark's Roman Catholic Parish

The Loving Legacy of Fr. Braun and Sr. Jeanne

For most of us, Msgr. Braun, Sr. Jeanne (and Sr. Kathleen!) are part of our families. Case in point: the Littlefield family photo album. Mary Pat Littlefield flipped through the family album and found dozens of photos of our beloved friends tucked in among the rest of the family, right where they belong.

A Buffalo Scrapbook: St. Mark's Roman Catholic Parish

They've been there for our lives… More from the Littlefield family album

The Loving Legacy of Fr. Braun and Sr. Jeanne

St. Marks School Held An Adventures In Science Day

St. Marks School hosted Adventures in Science Day on January 10th. Carol Rogers from the New York State Parks Interpretive Programs presented "Animals in Winter" to second grade students. From L to R: Patrick Dearing, Carol Rogers, Ken Chriswell, Erin O'Brien

St. Mark's School conducted its Fourth Annual Science Day on January 10th. It was an educational extravaganza chock full of visual opportunities, ideal for turning kids onto the world of science.

toric Preservation.

The presenters conducted live experiments, displayed animals and even demonstrated rocket science - all with the idea of exposing St. Mark's students to an array of scientific experts and

North Buffalo Rocket

The Loving Legacy of Fr. Braun and Sr. Jeanne

St. Mark Students smiling with Bishop Edward Head (above) and in the classroom (below)

A Buffalo Scrapbook: St. Mark's Roman Catholic Parish

A lover of sports and one who encouraged the passion and teamwork sports creates, Msgr. Braun's rare vacations often revolved around sports trips.

The Loving Legacy of Fr. Braun and Sr. Jeanne

From his coaching days at Bishop Turner, to Masses celebrating championships and victories for St. Mark teams, to his showing of Bills spirit with school kids or by ending Sunday Mass with a "Go Bills," Msgr. Braun was one of St. Mark's biggest sports fans.

A Buffalo Scrapbook: St. Mark's Roman Catholic Parish

Since Sr. Jeanne and Msgr. Braun placed so much of their focus on the children of St. Mark School, much of the portion of this book dedicated to celebrating and honoring Sr. Jeanne and Msgr. Braun will focus on

The Loving Legacy of Fr. Braun and Sr. Jeanne

those who have brought them so much pleasure and those who owe them so much—The Children of St. Mark School.

A Buffalo Scrapbook: St. Mark's Roman Catholic Parish

> Sister Jeanne Eberle (formerly Sr. Joan of Arc)
>
> I was the 2nd oldest of 10 children — 7 girls and 3 boys. We all went to St. Mary Magdalene School — we never would have been able to go there if they charged tuition. Sr. Mary Joan was my teacher in 5th & 6th Grade. On many Saturdays she asked me to accompany her to her ailing sister's house to help her clean. The friendship with Sr. Mary Joan, a kind, gentle woman, started me thinking about the convent.
>
> I went to Mt. St. Joseph Academy for high school — it was $100 a year. My Spanish teacher Sr. St. Leonard got me thinking again about the convent.
>
> When I graduated from high school, I knew that I wanted to be a teacher. D'Youville College was just beginning a Cadet Teacher Program in which the candidate taught 3 years in a Catholic School and two years of summers and college courses. So at the age of 17 I took one psychology course and a Methods course — right after high sch[ool]

Sr. Jeanne's handwritten autobiography

Both Sr. Jeanne and Msgr. Braun have spent decades collecting and saving the stories of St. Mark. Many of the school photos in this portion of the book were personally saved by Sister, and much of the history throughout was personally researched by Father. Wonderfully, both Msgr. Braun and Sr. Jeanne have made handwritten notes of some St. Mark history. The following pages are a transcription of an autobiography Sr. Jeanne wrote specifically for the research of this book.

The Loving Legacy of Fr. Braun and Sr. Jeanne

Sister Jeanne Eberle (formerly Sr. Joan of Arc)

I was the 2nd oldest of 10 children-- 7 girls and 3 boys. We all went to St. Mary Magdalene School-- we never would have been able to go there if they charged tuition. Sr. Mary Joan was my teacher in 5th and 6th grade. On many Saturdays she called me to accompany her to her ailing sister's house to help her clean. The friendship with Sr. Mary Joan, a kind, gentle woman, started me thinking about the convent.

I went to Mount St. Joseph Academy for high school-- it was $100 a year. My Spanish teacher, Sr. St. Leonard got me thinking again about the convent.

When I graduated from high school, I knew that I wanted to be a teacher. D'Youville College was just beginning a cadet teacher program, in which the candidate taught 3 years in a Catholic school and two years and summers of college courses.

So at the age of 17, I took one psychology course and a Methods course-- right after high school and "was prepared" to teach Grade 2 at St. Boniface School. For three years I taught there and took after-school classes, Saturday classes, and summer classes at D'Youville. For two years, we had one semester teaching and one semester at D'YC. Senior year was spent completely at D'YC.

When I graduated I took the Buffalo Public Schools exam and spent the next four years at School 48 on Best and Masten (Edna Place). I loved the children, the faculty and two great principals there. I received tenure after three years of teaching. The thought of the convent came coming back to me. So at the end of the 4th year, I entered the Sisters of St. Joseph.

Since I was an experienced teacher, I was assigned to teach at St. Vincent's-- the day after I entered. People on Main Street stopped traffic to look at me in my "penguin" postulant outfit. The 2nd year in the convent was the novitiate, in which we spent a year cleaning, scrubbing, doing dishes, waiting on the senior Sisters, etc, and praying. We spent much time each day learning about religious life.

One vivid memory-- One Friday, I was putting milk away in a huge walk-in refrigerator when I got locked in. The lights went out and there I was, stranded. I tried to find something to bang on to get someone's attention. My fingers went into gravy, Jell-o, mashed potatoes, etc. I finally realized there

A Buffalo Scrapbook: St. Mark's Roman Catholic Parish

was a huge milk can in there. I groped around for it, found it and a hammer. I started banging on it and I was freezing. At last, a worker heard the noise and rescued me. I was a half-hour late for evening prayers. The novice mistress had no compassion but gave me a penance (punishment) for being late for prayers. If the worker hadn't heard me, I would have been in there for three more hours.

Next year in convent was spent working on my Master's at State Teacher's College and Mount St. Joseph Teacher's College.

I spent one year teaching Grade 2 at St. Mark's. I had 55 children in my class. When the principal asked if I could take one more, I said, "Why not? What's the difference? 55 or 56?" There were no specials, classes like gym, art and music. Each grade had two classes with 48-56 in each class. Peg Brady was one of my stars. First Communion was quite a challenge with over 100 children.

In addition, the 1st and 2nd grade teachers had the privilege of cooking a big meal for the Sisters. Half of the faculty were lay people, half were sisters. Each night, the 1st grade teacher and I had to pack the makings of dinner in a big aluminum box and put it in the refrig. We had salad, raw potatoes, raw vegetables, and meat to prepare as well as dessert. After dinner we had to clean up the kitchen.

All the children went home for lunch. On feast days we had much more to prepare. What a memorable year!

There was no convent at that time-- we went back and forth from the Mount by cab. The two of us lucky people had to run up the stairs to get dinner going. Primary grades got out 15 minutes early so we could put on the finishing touches. It was a real challenge doing dinner and preparing for 56 youngsters.

The go-home taxi cab came about a half-hour after dismissal. We had to finish kitchen and get lessons prepared for the next day. As soon as we got home, we went to prayers!

We had the long habits, rosary, and cincture on at the time. Many times I caught the rosary and cincture on the desks-- the rows were very narrow. We had nine rows of desks.

Then I spent four years at Mt. St. Joseph Elementary School, and then started teaching Psychology and education courses (upstairs at Mount St. Joseph Teacher's College, now Medaille) on Saturdays and in the summer.

On July 4, 1960, I received the habit and my new name Sr. Joan of Arc. We could ask for three names-- my first choice was St Therese, since I had devotion to her. The novice mistress told me I didn't resemble a little flower-- so I got my patron saint, Joan of Arc.

A Buffalo Scrapbook: St. Mark's Roman Catholic Parish

Mount St. Joseph's name was changed to Medaille. I became full-time as an assistant professor. I began taking courses for my doctorate. One semester I took 26 credits at SUNYAB and was working full-time at the college. I became Director of the Education Division and the Graduate Division. I took a year off to write my dissertation, "A Descriptive Study of Teacher - Pupil Verbal Dyadic Interaction in the Informal Classroom."

I received my doctorate in Elementary and Remedial Instruction in 1978.

I spent two years as principal of St. Aloysius School, Cheektowaga. I loved the children and parents there. Some of them will be my lifelong friends.

In 1977, I chose to go to St. Mark's. The pastor was Fr. Robert Ochs, who was very supportive of the school. In 1980, Fr. Braun came. I can't say enough about him-- his support, his compassion, his generosity, his love for our students and youth.

I spent 34 great years with wonderful teachers, beautiful children and dedicated, hard-working parents. One of my first accomplishments was to begin the Home School Association. Previously, there had been little school involvement.

I gave my full blessings to Sharon McDermid who began our hot lunch program, swimming, cheerleading, volleyball, Ski Club, etc.

The Loving Legacy of Fr. Braun and Sr. Jeanne

Sr. Kathleen and I introduced the Talent Show which continued each year until she retired. It gave many children the opportunity to shine before an audience. It encouraged many youngsters to become interested in music or drama. Their interest is continuing today. One of the most remembered shows was the "Debutante" act. Fathers of children in school and parishioners dressed in tutus and performed a ballet. The act brought down the house.

Another memorable talent show was when a number of the faculty and poor principal acted out "Sister Act" dressed in modified habits.

During Advent, we had a Family Mass followed by entertainment in the Gym. Parents and students had a number of practices beforehand. We acted out the "12 Days of Christmas" one year, "Twas the Night Before Christmas" another year. We had tons of fun, having 70-80 people on stage at the same time.

Sr. Kathleen and I brought St. Mark's into the technological world by installing our first computers-- Apple IIe. We taught Logo-- how to program. We took a computer class at Canisius. We did complicated projects-- mine was programming national flags of many different countries. We completed them at 3:00am the night before it was due. Several people wondered why the lights were on in the computer room that late.

A Buffalo Scrapbook: St. Mark's Roman Catholic Parish

For years I was the #1 fan of our sports teams, until I became old and feeble and mowed down with too many things to do. My favorite sport was basketball with Kevin Spitler as coach. One red-letter day was when we won the Diocesan Championship against OLV. We were down by 11 points with about one-and-a-half minutes to go. I had told Kevin before the game to pray to the angels which he did. At the end of the game, I went to the Catholic Store and bought angel pins for the team. We celebrated with pizza and pins.

We had many rallies for the Bills. On one occasion the teachers painted me up. After the rally, I had hoped to "fly" to Brockport, where my father was dying. The phone rang and it was a mother dying of cancer. I talked to her for at least an hour. We took off with my "Bills" face and outfit still on. My father waited to die until we got there.

A few things I did for 34 years--

1.) Stayed in school almost every night until 10 or 10:30. (I do miss that.)

2.) Wrote welcome notes to Kindergarten children and new children entering the school.

3.) Helped needy families at Christmas giving them presents and food. Many families contributed to this project and the goodies were given to the families anonymously.

4.) Also helped families who lost their jobs.

5.) Wrote Christmas letters to all the students in the school. The children thought they were hand-written. Don't tell them I put them on the copy

A Buffalo Scrapbook: St. Mark's Roman Catholic Parish

machine. It was a real challenge to prepare the letters and wrap up a little gift for each child when we had over 390 students.

6.) I honored the children who earned 1st Honors all year by giving them a small gold cup at the end-of-the year Mass.

7.) I spent a great deal of time "counseling" students who had family problems or peer-related problems. I know I was instrumental in preventing a suicide.

8.) I always tried to be available to parents, students, and faculty.

9.) My real success story is with a 2nd grade boy who came to St. Mark's after being expelled from another Catholic school. Our first year was a real experience. He climbed up walls in the lav, ran out of the front door of the school often with me chasing after him. Mrs. Riordan, the second grade teacher, was extremely patient with him. Said he would be a lawyer of doctor someday. He graduated from St. Mark's and I'm proud to say in June 2012, he graduated from UB Medical School.

10.) I have a story about an 8th grader who was going to jump off the building. I don't think it's so good to write about it.

11.) Sr. Kathleen and I organized the Christmas pageant every year, 2013 being the last one. She did the music; I did the speaking parts of the pageant. It was a JOY!

12.) I felt very privileged to prepare children for First Communion each year.

A Buffalo Scrapbook: St. Mark's Roman Catholic Parish

I worked without school children and with the CCD children from public school.

It truly was a gift to serve God's people as a Sister of St. Joseph for 54 years and as principal of St. Mark's for 34 years. I felt very much at home at St. Mark's-- I will remember the children and loving parents forever.

I received three awards which I didn't deserve. I just did my job and tried to make a difference in children's lives.

Awards: Ned Mathias Award- "Unsung Hero"- given by the West Side Rowing Club- 2007.

Bishop's Medal presented by Bishop Kmiec in 2008.

Woman of Influence Award from Business First in 2009.

Right now, and for almost two years, I have been volunteering three mornings of the week at Gerard Place, helping unwed mothers and others in the community to prepare for the GED. A few weeks ago, we were privileged to have four immigrants from the Congo come to us. They were all educated in Africa but their English is extremely limited. It is a challenge to try to communicate with them. It is more difficult than teaching kindergarten children.

The Loving Legacy of Fr. Braun and Sr. Jeanne

A Buffalo Scrapbook: St. Mark's Roman Catholic Parish

From 95th Anniversary booklet:
Since St. Mark's inception, the quality and integrity of our members have set St. Mark's apart. Today's parishioners continue to foster a supportive Christian community, and further the goals of our church and school.

St. Mark students are always full of spirit, for Buffalo and for St. Mark.

A Buffalo Scrapbook: St. Mark's Roman Catholic Parish

—*News Staff Photographer Robert L. Smith*

SUBS SURFACE — Turnabout was fair play at St. Mark's School Monday, as students learned that bread cast upon the waters is likely to come back in the form of submarine sandwiches. The eighth-grade class that recently donated its $200 class luncheon money to a teacher who'd had a string of misfortunes was treated in turn by faculty members who launched a sub sandwich lunch at the school. Sister Jeanne Eberle, left, the school principal, and teacher Lucy Beatty prepare to serve the first sub to Nancy Morrison, 13, as the rest of the kids wait their turns.

From The Buffalo Evening News, 1979

Monday Night Bingo proceeds are used for the teachers' financial incentives. Friday Night proceeds support a substantial percentage of the school's finances. *From a 1985 parish report.*

A Buffalo Scrapbook: St. Mark's Roman Catholic Parish

Msgr. Braun's handwritten history of St. Mark's

Over the century that St. Mark has called North Buffalo home, there has been no greater steward of the parish's history than Msgr. Braun. His private tours of the church, peppered with color and passion, were always high-bid items when offered at events like Lionheart. Only days before he said goodbye as the pastor of St. Mark, he gave one final tour.

The following pages are a transcription of the tour filled with the kind of detail only Fr. Braun could give.

The Loving Legacy of Fr. Braun and Sr. Jeanne

Msgr. Braun's Tour of St. Mark's

The first church was a wooden church, built about where the hedge is out in front of the side door of the school. The Rectory was built next, then this church was built, then the school. Bell tower added about 20 years later.

The first pastor, John McMahon, had it in his plans, but he had a parishioner who told him a bell tower would just be a pain in the neck. He had money—he owned a silk mill—so he told Fr. McMahon, "if you don't build a bell tower, I'll donate the altars."

McMahon agreed to it, so there was no bell tower initially in 1914 when the church was built. By 1920, the silk mill owner had died, McMahon was leaving here, and was looking to get in the good graces of Rome.

It was the time of the rise of dictators like Mussolini and Hitler, and in 1925, the Church had established the Feast of Christ the King, as a counter balance to fight the idea that a dictator could be God-like. The idea was *"Christ* is the King, not Mussolini."

The bell tower wound up being the first edifice in the North America dedicated to Christ the King. Fr. McMahon was named Bishop of Trenton, NJ by Pope Pius XI shortly thereafter.

A Buffalo Scrapbook: St. Mark's Roman Catholic Parish

PASTOR — REV. FRANCIS BRAUN

Bishop McMahon had a heart condition. He was visiting his physician brother in South Buffalo around Christmas time, and went to Mercy Hospital for a check-up. Before the check-up, he went into the chapel to say Mass, and he keeled over and died in the chapel of a heart attack.

The three altars are all made of white marble, the two side altars and the main altar.

The windows above the main altar are the Evangelists-- the Gospel writers. The first one is Mark with the lion, then Matthew. On the right is John with the eagle, and Luke with the ox.

The Loving Legacy of Fr. Braun and Sr. Jeanne

The statues are the only remaining pieces of the old, original wooden 1908 St. Mark church. Joseph, Anthony, the Sacred Heart of Jesus, and Mary. Everything else was new for the current church, which was started in 1914, and finished over the next few years.

Little touches prove St. Mark was built as an Irish parish.

The St. Anthony statue to the right of the main altar is an Irish representation of the saint. Usually, the Italian representation of the saint shows him holding the baby Jesus. The Irish version shows him holding a book, because he was the first teacher of the Franciscans, and the piece of bread in his hand shows his hospitality and generosity.

At the time the church was built, the favorite saints were St. Anthony and St. Theresa, and there's a St. Theresa statue at the side door.

They were all Irish, but they had statues of the Portuguese St. Anthony and the French St. Theresa. In the earliest days, there was never a St. Patrick statue in the church.

The name of St. Mark Church was picked out by Bishop Charles Colton. In January, 1908, the bishop wrote to a priest in Ellicottville, Fr. Edward Rengel, asking him if he wished to come build a parish he was planning to start in North Buffalo-- further saying he had envisioned that it was to become a very elite part of the city. In the letter, Bishop Colton said he'd name the new parish either Epiphany or St. Mark.

Well he didn't come, but Father John McMahon did come from Fly Street in the Hooks, in April 1908. He became the first pastor. He was a native of Cuba, NY, and he'd been a priest for about ten years when he came here.

Originally, the rectory was just a plain wood frame house. In 1921, they added the stone work, to make it look like a castle. That stonework is in no way practical. It was also eventually expanded in the back-- the original house only went back about half as far, to where the side door is now.

The stained glass is the work of Otto Andrle, a retired actor from Switzerland.

A Buffalo Scrapbook: St. Mark's Roman Catholic Parish

His plans for the windows were to chronologically trace Jesus' life. Starting with the Bethlehem window, the conception-- Mary with Gabriel, then Jesus offered in the Temple at about a month old. The next window was going to be Jesus at 12 in the temple, and the last window is him just beginning his public life as teacher at Cana. All these scenes are indoors.

On the other side, they were all supposed to be outdoors, with the theme, "Jesus in activity." The first is Jesus as shepherd, then Jesus as a healer, then the third window is Jesus as a teacher-- which is actually the window that's on the right-- with Jesus teaching the young children. The last window is Jesus teaching the apostles, and the final is the resurrection window. They are all outdoors, and all Jesus as an active adult.

The parishioners revolted against his plan. They wanted a hospitality window, showing Martha welcoming Jesus at her house. She lived outside Bethlehem with her brother Lazarus and sister Mary, and every time Jesus would go to Bethlehem, Jesus would stop at her house for a meal.

When Andrle told them he couldn't fit it into his plans, the response, in essence was, if you don't fit it in, you don't get paid.

So the artist had to move a few things around. He moved the teaching window across, wiping out the window of Jesus in the temple.

Andrle's trademark was to include a hat and a cane in his windows. It's in the first window to the left of the altar.

The back window is St. Cecila, the patron saint of singers. She's holding a harpsichord. Then, in each section, there are four angels. The angels next to her are holding a scroll; they are the first Latin words to the shortest of the psalms.

St. Mark was hit twice when vandals were throwing rocks through stained glass windows around the city around 1990.

The Loving Legacy of Fr. Braun and Sr. Jeanne

In one way it was a compliment that they came here, because they only hit the good churches, like St. Louis, Westminster Presbyterian, First Episcopal. The first hit was the shepherd's window, and the local company that repaired it, and still had the original "cartoons"—Andrle's plans for the windows.

If you look closely at the shepherd's window, you'll see grayish sheep and one

A Buffalo Scrapbook: St. Mark's Roman Catholic Parish

whitish sheep. That's where there window was broken.

The second time, they hit the upper right hand corner of the front window. It was after these two strikes of vandalism that lexan plastic sheets were installed over all the stained glass windows.

Overall, the English Gothic design and style of the church would be more fitting at Cambridge or Oxford. The people who started the church were Irish, and the new parish would be made up of 40-50 families and 70-80 servants, as mentioned in Bishop Colton's letter to Fr. Rengel.

At the time, the neighborhoods surrounding the church were made up of mostly Presbyterian and Episcopalian families. Many of those upper class Protestants didn't want a Catholic church and the influx of most lower class Irish it would likely draw. But in many cases, the Irish were already in those homes, as butlers, maids, and groomsmen for the horses. In many Parkside and Central Park homes, these servants lived on the third floor, which was accessed by its own separate staircase in the kitchen.

By the time St. Mark was built, the seemingly more appropriate Irish Gothic look was already represented in the low-slung stone look at The Episcopal Church of the Good Shepherd. The thought was, if they have our look, then we'll take theirs, and build a church that looks a lot like an Episcopal church.

They wanted to build in Lewis Bennett's development, and they inquired about the island at Starin, Morris, and Linden. When Bennett designed Central Park, he created those islands, and intended that churches should be built on them-- like Parkside Lutheran.

Bennett refused to sell, saying there'd be no Catholic church in his development.

The only lots available were the four on the corner of Amherst and Woodward.

The tough early parishioners of St. Mark built a church right away. In most cases, a parish would build a combination church/school first, then build the permanent church later. You can see that at Holy Spirit, St. Margaret's, and St. Rose. You originally had one building with one floor for the church and the second floor for the school.

The Loving Legacy of Fr. Braun and Sr. Jeanne

At St. Mark, they built the first wooden church in 1908, the permanent church in 1914, and then built the school in 1920.

How has the Mass changed through the years?

For the first ten years of my priesthood, you said Mass only at the marble altar, and you said Mass facing the tabernacle. You'd turn around to say, "The Lord be with you" to the people, but for everything else your back was to the people, until you came down to proclaim the Gospel. The gospel was in English, but everything else was in Latin. Every weekend had a set Gospel, they never changed. Most of them were from St. Matthew. A priest would face the altar, there was a big Mass book that would be on the right hand side, which he'd just read in Latin. People would follow along in their own missal, written in English. They could follow what he was saying, but they'd never hear him say it.

He'd have the first reading-- the only reading-- and the psalm on the right hand side, and then the altar boy would take the book down and carry it around to the left hand side for him to read the Gospel in Latin. The Epistle Side and the Gospel Side.

Then he would come to the pulpit and proclaim the gospel in English. These were the days before bulletins, too, so the priest would make any announcements, then the sermon.

It put a lot more on the priest; there was more public activity, and being clear in your English and so on. In the old days, in Latin, you could really just mumble it along. You were really the only one who knew what you were saying.

Some of the older priests objected, some were very happy to have the changes. Just like the changes to the missal happening now. Some are happy for the new words, some aren't. Like me now, I'm glad I'm getting out before they change up the Mass again.

Everything at St. Mark is virtually the same from those days. The pulpit is still there, but not used. Obviously they added the wooden altar table, and there used to be an altar rail. The rail went across the front of the altar. It had a door, but that door was always closed. So for Communion, people would come up and kneel at the altar rail, and receive Communion kneeling down. If you look at the stairs leading to the altar, that wide second step is meant to

133

kneel on, with your feet resting on the bottom step.

The priest would walk along the rail and give people the Eucharist. You really needed servers in those days for the changing of the book, the ringing of the bells, and the holding of the paten for Communion. They'd always be holding a plate under the person's chin as they received Communion.

The only other change to the altar is there used to be a big long chain coming down from the ceiling over the altar with a red light at the bottom. That was the sanctuary lamp. We have a more portable one on the altar now, but then, it would hang about 6 feet above where people could reach.

When the church was first built, there were only the three main doors at the back. When fire laws changed, they wound up adding the side door onto Amherst Street.

The pulpit was done by a woodworking outfit in the Old Spaghetti Warehouse building-- EM Hager & Sons Woodmill. Hager was in charge of the crafting of the pulpit. The pulpit was primarily needed because of acoustics. In big churches, the pulpit was often a quarter of the way down the aisle. When it was added, half of a front pew was removed.

The Loving Legacy of Fr. Braun and Sr. Jeanne

The pulpit was hand-carved, and made from one single piece of wood. Each design is carved right into the single piece of wood. Before we discovered that the pulpit was just one piece, we had hoped to be able to move the top part over for a lectern, and use the base as a for an enthronement for the gospel book. So now, it's really only used twice a year. Once during the kids' Mass at Christmas, when the angel hides in the pulpit and then pops up to say, "I bring you good news of great joy," and then on Palm Sunday, the third reader will stand up there. So it's not so useful, but it is beautiful. To remove it would take away from the beauty, appearance, and style of the church, even though I could never use it. To me, it feels like the king talking to the peasants in the Wizard of Id comic strip. It's not the procedure you'd want at all today for the presentation of liturgy.

It was at the same time the pulpit was added that the St. Theresa statue was added, and the same outfit did the work.

Also in the beginning, the baptismal font was in the little room that is now a confessional. The custom in those days was the Godparents would bring the baby, and the parents would stay at home. Five or six babies and their godparents would line up, and when it was time to pour the water on the baby's head, they'd go into the room, and so on. With the new liturgy of Vatican II, baptism was made public, and that's when the font moved to the altar on the right.

In the old days, you just had Mass in the morning. You couldn't have Mass after 12. Masses would go from 6 in the morning 'til noon, then in the afternoon, you'd have baptisms. And on Saturday night-- no one had heard of Mass on a Saturday night. That's when they'd have confessions from say 3-5, and then from 7-9. The tradition was then that you did not receive Communion unless you went to confession the night before. And if you were going to Communion in the morning, you couldn't eat after midnight. Not even to drink water. So with that Communion fast, the first two masses, say at 6, 7, or 8, you always had a lot of people going to Communion. If you had Mass at 9, 10, or 11, you had very few people going to Communion because they had broken their fasts. Many times in those late Masses, the priest would be the only one taking Communion. In the late 40's, they relaxed the fast so you could drink water.

That's why the guilds and holy names would have monthly Communions-- to make sure people would get Communion once a month, anyway.

St. Mark Altar, 1950s.

The altar carving shows Jesus from the Book of Revelation as the conquering the Passover lamb.

As far as altar decoration-- usually the altar is filled with candles and flowers. It's just personal preference, but I've never been a fan of flowers. So for the 100th anniversary of the parish, I put up paintings by long time parishioner Marge Norton on the altar. There's a flag that was brought home from Baghdad, and I also keep the patches of the guys and girls who are serving now in the Army, Navy, Air Force, Marines, and Coast Guard.

The Loving Legacy of Fr. Braun and Sr. Jeanne

Using windows as teaching opportunity

In the Middle Ages and before, and even into the early 1900s, most Catholics and most people in general, were uneducated. They couldn't read. The windows are now and were then a presentation of the Bible that everyone could understand. Every church had windows, like a comic strip-- to educate the people on certain scenes. They were beautiful to look at and told the stories so well.

The windows were created to emphasize people's knowledge of the Bible. Today, there's less of a need. We have a three year rotation of readings, and of course, people can read; they're educated. But in those old days, these images were there to remind you of Jesus the Shepherd, Jesus the Healer, and so on.

And these windows here are beautiful. St. James, where I grew up in Kensington-Bailey, had lousy windows. They were plain and just painted over.

Up in the loft, the original organ was a pump organ. In 1940, they made into an electric organ. The pipes you see serve no purpose; they were left to conceal empty space.

In 1914, the church was built for gas light. The four lights on each side were the only lights. To bring in more light, where the ceiling begins at the back of the church, they removed a few stones to create a catwalk above the ceiling, so that the lights can be changed from above.

I've looked in, but have never been in the catwalk. The fans were added after that.

A Buffalo Scrapbook: St. Mark's Roman Catholic Parish

As the tour wrapped up, something reminded Msgr. Braun about Fr. Kirchmeyer, a priest at his boyhood parish, St. James.

The first time my mother when to him for confession, she spent about ten minutes in the confessional, and then he told her, 'Ok, you've told me all your husband's sins... Now what are yours?' Oh, she was mad! She never went back to him for confession. She worked with him, was very active in the parish, but she never went to confession with him again.

My dad was very formal, very concise, very orderly. He worked downtown for Customs. He went to confession every week, but he'd go to St. Michael's for confession. One time it was Christmas time, and as he walked into our home church confessional, the door slammed behind him. Fr. Kirchmeyer yelled at him, 'If you came more than once a year, you'd know how to close the door right!'

Msgr. Braun as a little boy, left.

Buffalo Evening News, 1959

Fr. Braun's dad's obituary. As you read through his life and the names of his family, how many different Fr. Braun stories and homilies are you reminded of?

Note the former Mary Hennessy, "who had a beautiful Irish name, and gave it up for a dark German name."

GEORGE A. BRAUN DIES; VETERAN OF CUSTOMS SERVICE

George A. Braun, 66, retired assistant deputy customs collector at Niagara Falls for several years, died Monday (Oct. 19, 1959) in Sisters' Hospital.

A heart attack caused Mr. Braun's retirement from active duty about a year ago. He was taken to the hospital Monday.

In the Customs Service for 42 years, his career covered duties as administrator in the Federal Office Bldg. here for many years, as an inspector on Buffalo-area international bridges and aboard foreign travel ships and on railroad trains.

He ws a charter member of the Men's Club of St. Ann's Parish. He attended St. James Church and was a member of its Holy Name Society. He also was a member of the Columban Retreat League and of George F. Lamm Post, 622, American Legion.

Mr. Braun is survived by his wife, the former Mary A. Hennessy; four sons, the Rev. G. Francis, assistant pastor of St. Benedict's Church, Eggertsville, currently in Rome on the North American Pilgrimage; the Rev. John J., WF, missionary to Africa and now studying at the Gregorian University, Rome; Navy Specialist 3/C Jerome N., stationed in Newport, R. I., and Paul at homes.

Also surviving are two daughters, Miss Mary Ann Braun, a teacher in nursing in St. Joseph's Hospital, Chicago, and Mrs. William Crittenden, Town of Tonawanda; two brothers, Norbert J., and Arthur J., and a sister, Mrs. Edward Goatseay.

A Buffalo Scrapbook: St. Mark's Roman Catholic Parish

The Loving Legacy of Fr. Braun and Sr. Jeanne

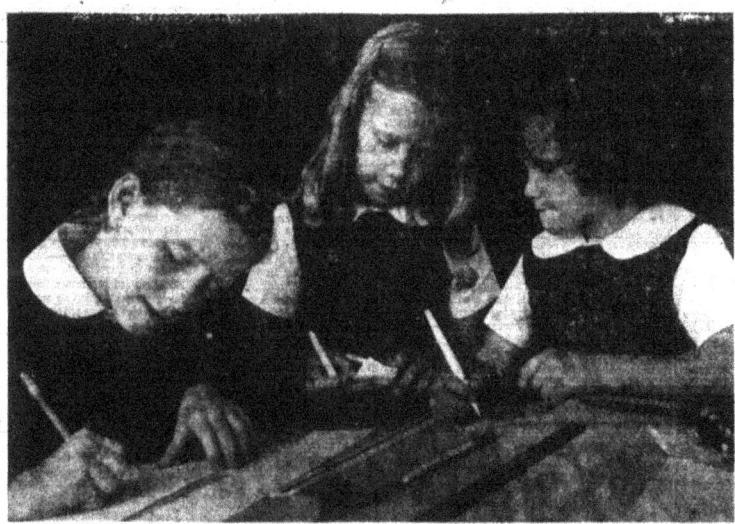

ALL IN THE FAMILY — The sisters Brinkworth, from left, Ellen, 12; DeeDee, 8, and Kate, 5, work on a project for Catholic Schools Week, which starts tomorrow with the theme, "The Catholic School, One of the Family." The Brinkworth girls attend St. Mark's School at 399 Woodward Ave.

Pontiff's Message Set the Stage For Catholic Schools Week in State

Catholic Schools Week in New York State begins tomorrow, and the event couldn't have had a more timely send-off than the one provided by Pope John Paul II.

"We were thrilled that the pope spoke so strongly in affirming the value of Catholic education when he spoke to those teen-agers in New York," said Monsignor John M. Ryan, superintendent of schools in the Diocese of Buffalo.

The message boosted morale of parents and school officials alike at a time of tremendous financial pressure on the schools.

The diocese on Oct. 28 will kick off an unprecedented one-week drive to raise funds to support the 10 diocesan high schools.

* * *

THE CAMPAIGN will emphasize that Catholic schools are saving the taxpayer tremendous amounts of money. The State Education Department estimates it costs an average $3,036 to educate a student in a public school.

Based on that rate, the diocesan high schools save the public $13 million, Monsignor Ryan said. All the Western New York Catholic schools combined save an estimated $130 million that would otherwise have to be raised in taxes, he said.

The theme of Catholic Schools Week is "The Catholic School, One of the Family."

Monsignor Ryan said the theme means the religious training provided in Catholic schools should be considered as essential a part of a youngster's upbringing as the guidance provided by his parents and other family members.

SCHOOLS WEEK will conclude Oct. 21 with a special Mass offered by Bishop Edward D. Head in St. Joseph's Old Cathedral. Students from the diocesan high schools will assist as trumpeters, folk musicians and gift bearers.

But the individual schools themselves will be the center of most of the celebrations.

Open house programs will be held tomorrow at St. Joseph's Collegiate Institute and St. Aloysius School and Wednesday at Mount St. Mary Academy. Schools such as Holy Spirit, Our Lady of Czestochowa, St. Josaphat, Queen of Martyrs and St. Elizabeth's will hold special liturgical services or Masses.

Other events include displays of student artwork at Our Lady of Czestochowa and St. Barnabas, the launching of balloons containing scriptural messages, talent shows, discussions of social and religious issues and parent night and grandparent night programs.

Buffalo Evening News, 1979

A Buffalo Scrapbook: St. Mark's Roman Catholic Parish

The children of St. Mark School are also at home in St. Mark church.

The Loving Legacy of Fr. Braun and Sr. Jeanne

A Buffalo Scrapbook: St. Mark's Roman Catholic Parish

The Loving Legacy of Fr. Braun and Sr. Jeanne

Since the 1970s, Sister Kathleen Barrett has been an integral part of the St. Mark community, teaching 4th Grade, acting as Assistant Principal, generally being Sr. Jeanne's constant companion, and being friend to one and all.

A Buffalo Scrapbook: St. Mark's Roman Catholic Parish

A long standing tradition for the parish: The children acting out the Christmas Vigil Mass.

The Loving Legacy of Fr. Braun and Sr. Jeanne

A Buffalo Scrapbook: St. Mark's Roman Catholic Parish

Sister Kathleen and Sister Jeanne would spend weeks preparing with the children… And dozens of St. Mark newborns have had the honor of playing the infant Jesus during the Mass.

The Loving Legacy of Fr. Braun and Sr. Jeanne

Fr. Ochs, Fr. Clody, Fr. Braun, and Fr. Joe have all celebrated the Mass.

A Buffalo Scrapbook: St. Mark's Roman Catholic Parish

"Field trips are centered around cultural or educational themes, and are conducted at various intervals during the year." 1985 parish report

The Loving Legacy of Fr. Braun and Sr. Jeanne

ST. MARK'S TEACHER HONORED

Educator of Excellence Mr. Cecala, with 7th graders Lindsay Bonn (left), Dan McCarthy and Jamila Lee.

Frank P. Cecala, teacher of English and Drama at St. Mark's School and director of Theatre at Amherst Central High School has been named an Educator of Excellence by the New York State English Council.

Teachers and administrators in English and Language Arts from all over New York State were nominated by submissions that supported excellence and this year's conference theme, "NYSEC 2000: Where Past and Future Intersect." Frank's nomination portfolio included recommendations by an administrator, a teaching colleague, and a student, as well as samples of exemplar teaching materials.

Frank received this award recently at NYSEC's Annual Conference in Albany. The conference drew almost one thousand English Language Arts teachers and administrators from across the State.

A former honoree, Mr. Cecala had received this award from the Council for Excellence in the Teaching of English and Drama/Theatre at the 1980 conference. Since retiring from the Buffalo Public Schools after 36 years as a teacher of English, Frank decided to continue teaching and second year as a teacher of and Theatre at St. Mark's.

Msgr. Braun poses with kids… and hardware.

The Loving Legacy of Fr. Braun and Sr. Jeanne

WEDNESDAY, MARCH 31, 1999

St. Marks Basketball Team Rewrites School History

Pictured form L to R: Megan Dearing, Rachel Perillo, Meggie Knapp, Faith Huffnagle, Adrianne Mattina Row 2: Tom Johnson, coach; Maria Pirrami, Caitlin Corr, Katherine Hohnson, Anna Nagro, Meg O'Sullivan; Joe Jagro, coach

After a Successful year with 32 wins and 3 losses, the Lady Lions complete an outstanding season which included 5 championships: W.N.Y. Catholic Girls Elementary Champs - Large School Division, Ken-Ton/Metro Champs, Hilbert College Tournament Champs, Kiwanis Tournament Champs, and Villa Maria Tournament Champs.

The pride of North Buffalo demonstrated the true spirit of the game with hard work, determination and dedication. At the core of their success was their selfless play, devotion to each other, and self-sacrifice. They set an example of unity and purpose that should inspire the whole community. The dedicated parent-coaches and young ladies are a perfect example of what St. Mark's is all about.

Buffalo Rocket

St. Mark's Team Has Undefeated Season

pictured left to right; First Row - Kevin Fanning, Peter Bertola, Tom Gilbert, Charles Siminski, Mark Mendola, Pat O'Rourke, Tim Lyons, Joe Crangle. Second Row - Coach Brion Neary, Paul Becher, Keith Stafford, Joel Campagna, Hank Nowak, Peter Littlefield, Steve McGoldrick, Darren Diggs, Peter Galvin, Assistant coach Jim Rath.

St. Mark's Boys Basketball Team had a successful season with a remarkable record of 10-0. Their undefeated season merited the Bishop Smith League championship. The Lions defeated St. Roses's, St. Josehp's, St. Margaret's, All Saints and St. Mary's School for the Deaf.

The Lions won second place in the Christ the King Tournament, defeating St. Joseph's, Niagara Falls, and Blessed Sacrament, Kenmore, in two close games. They received a beautiful trophy for their fine achievement. Peter Galvin and Hank Nowak were chosen as All-Star and received plaques.

A great deal of credit for the successful season goes to Coach Brion Neary from Canisius College, whose outstanding coaching led the team to the playoffs and to the tournaments. The Lions will never forget the concern he had for each of them, the enthusiasm he brought to every game, the many long hours he spent with them.

The Buffalo Rocket - April 28, 1982

A Buffalo Scrapbook: St. Mark's Roman Catholic Parish

Since the beginning of the home computer age in the early 1980s, Sr. Jeanne and Msgr. Braun committed to having current computer labs and instruction for the students of St. Mark.

Two different generations of St. Mark students on two different generations of St. Mark computers.

A Buffalo Scrapbook: St. Mark's Roman Catholic Parish

While Msgr. Braun says he's never used a computer, "and never will," Sr. Jeanne and Sr. Kathleen have stayed at the forefront of computer education.

Sr. Jeanne has even acted as an online cop. As the social media craze started taking off in 2006, The Buffalo News reported that Sr. Jeanne "busted a group of junior high students who had faked their ages so they could post on My Space," saying some switched their ages to 26 and 27.

A Buffalo Scrapbook: St. Mark's Roman Catholic Parish

A high standard of education has brought distinction to both teachers and pupils, many the graduates achieving flattering records in Catholic High Schools and Colleges of the Diocese, as well as in institutions of learning both in our country and abroad...

The Loving Legacy of Fr. Braun and Sr. Jeanne

These noted successes were due to the unique ability of the children, the loyal co-operation of the parents, but most of all, to the ability and untiring efforts of the Sisters of St. Joseph.
From a 1940s History of the Parish

A Buffalo Scrapbook: St. Mark's Roman Catholic Parish

St. Mark School staff and faculty.

The Loving Legacy of Fr. Braun and Sr. Jeanne

What better way to celebrate your First Communion than with a photo with Sr. Jeanne?

Sr. Jeanne took hundreds of First Communion photos in her 34 years at St. Mark.

A Buffalo Scrapbook: St. Mark's Roman Catholic Parish

These girls have St. Mark spirit enough to share…

The Loving Legacy of Fr. Braun and Sr. Jeanne

A Buffalo Scrapbook: St. Mark's Roman Catholic Parish

The Loving Legacy of Fr. Braun and Sr. Jeanne

While Sr. Jeanne and Msgr. Braun remain big supporters of sports like basketball at St. Mark, coaches from the community—like Kevin Spitler, Paul Smaldone and countless others—have been the backbone of these programs.

A Buffalo Scrapbook: St. Mark's Roman Catholic Parish

There is always time for smiles and for prayer at St. Mark

The Loving Legacy of Fr. Braun and Sr. Jeanne

BUFFALO ROCKET   WEDNESDAY OCTOBER 17, 1979

FAMILY FOLK MASS - was held at St. Mark's School to begin its celebration of Catholic Schools Week last Sunday. A Folk Group of fifth, sixth, seventh and eighth grade students led the singing. Readings were done by Caroline and Cathleen Vossler, 8th grade students, and Henry Bennett, a 4th grader. Family posters were displayed in the gym, made by the children in each of the families.

Fr. Braun at his normal station at the start of the school day... Greeting all of the children on their way into St. Mark. (WNY Catholic Weekly)

A Buffalo Scrapbook: St. Mark's Roman Catholic Parish

The Sharon McDermid Dining Room at St. Mark, named in honor of the woman who brought the hot lunch program and sports such as swimming

The Loving Legacy of Fr. Braun and Sr. Jeanne

to St. Mark, died at the age of 53 in 1996. During her too-short life, her dedication and volunteerism had an impact still seen today.

A Buffalo Scrapbook: St. Mark's Roman Catholic Parish

St. Mark's Children's Night

On Thursday, Oct. 18, St. Mark's third annual Children's Night will be held. A variety of activities will take place in each of the classrooms from 7-8:30, followed by refreshments provided by the Home-School Assoc. The activities will include short skits in which kindergarteners tell the story of various fairy tales, action songs, radio plays relating to Social Studies, Super Quiz, choral speaking and animal puppetry. Parents will test their scientific knowledge at the "Science Carnival" in Grade 7, and will be asked to participate in Values Clarification exercises in Grade 8, and in readings of students' original poetry and other creative writing.

The public is invited to attend.

Whether it was a Talent Show, a Spring Concert, a Christmas Pageant, or some other way to keep children involved and entertained, chances were pretty good that Sr. Jeanne and Sr. Kathleen were helping kids cook up something great!

The Loving Legacy of Fr. Braun and Sr. Jeanne

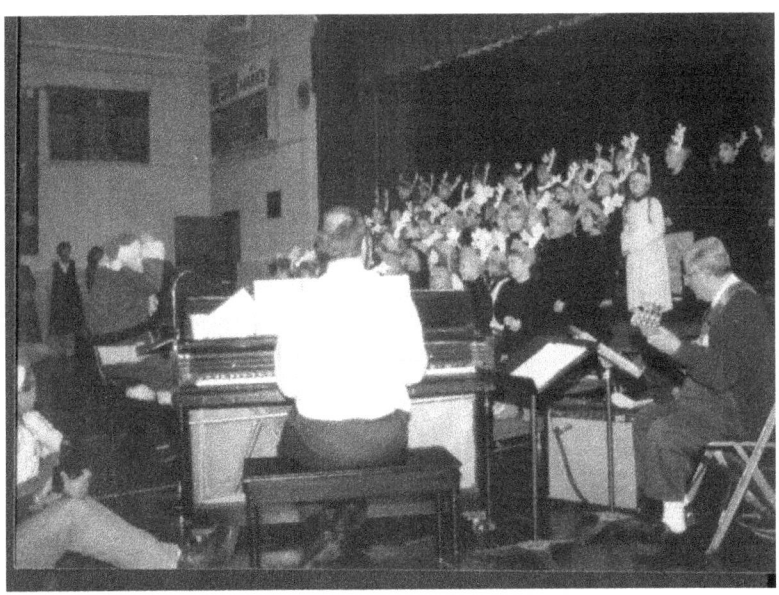

A Buffalo Scrapbook: St. Mark's Roman Catholic Parish

Celebrating St. Patrick's Day and marching in the St. Patrick's Day Parade have both been long-standing traditions of St. Mark Parish. (Notice the boarded-up building behind the parade... It's now The Mansion on Delaware Avenue luxury hotel.)

The Loving Legacy of Fr. Braun and Sr. Jeanne

A Buffalo Scrapbook: St. Mark's Roman Catholic Parish

The tradition is a long standing one which continues to this day.

The Loving Legacy of Fr. Braun and Sr. Jeanne

A Buffalo Scrapbook: St. Mark's Roman Catholic Parish

Some of the ladies of St. Mark School: Mrs. Amico, Miss Manne, Sr. Jeanne, Mrs. Vizzi

A Buffalo Scrapbook: St. Mark's Roman Catholic Parish

Officially, Miss Bridget Manne was the school secretary for 21 years. But as any student from the late 1980s to the late 2000s will tell you, she was much more than that. "She touched everybody's lives in every way possible," Sr. Jeanne told the Buffalo News when she died at the age of 87 in 2009. "She was the secretary, but nurse and counselor too—taking care of the kids when they were sick and counseling them when they were sad."

The Loving Legacy of Fr. Braun and Sr. Jeanne

Miss Manne with Bishop Mansell. She came to work at St. Mark after retiring from Hengerer's, where she worked for 46 years.

A Buffalo Scrapbook: St. Mark's Roman Catholic Parish

Another long-standing St. Mark School tradition: The Annual Halloween Parade

The Loving Legacy of Fr. Braun and Sr. Jeanne

Whether dressed as a clown, a football player, or heaven knows what, Sr. Kathleen was always ready for the Halloween Parade.

A Buffalo Scrapbook: St. Mark's Roman Catholic Parish

Before coming to St. Mark, Fr. Braun was much beloved at Bishop Turner High School.

The Loving Legacy of Fr. Braun and Sr. Jeanne

In his 17 years at Turner, Fr. Braun taught English and Religion and was a guidance counselor, coach, and Activities Director.

If you can judge a teacher by how many times his photo appears in the school yearbook, Fr. Braun was definitely among the most beloved teachers anywhere, with dozens of great shots of a beloved teacher through the years.

And it wasn't just the kids who loved him. Fr. Braun was honored by Bishop Edward Head as one of the outstanding teachers in the Diocesan school system in 1978.

A Buffalo Scrapbook: St. Mark's Roman Catholic Parish

All photos from Bishop Turner High School Year Books.

Fr. Francis Braun, Guidance Counselor, extolling the virtues of his alma mater, St. Bonaventure University.

A Buffalo Scrapbook: St. Mark's Roman Catholic Parish

Whether it's honoring the sacrifice of the War of 1812 soldiers buried under the Delaware Park Golf Course by planting flags (above) or mentioning them in homilies… or celebrating the history of our parish… or talking of how Old Buffalo impacts us today… or relating our lives to Biblical times… Fr. Braun constantly shared his love of history with us at St. Mark.

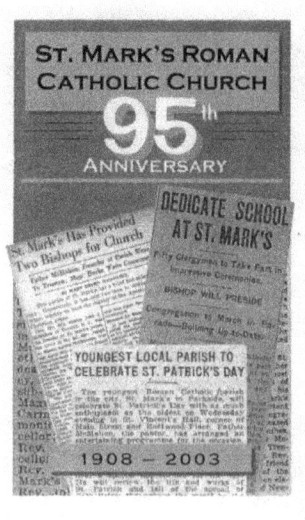

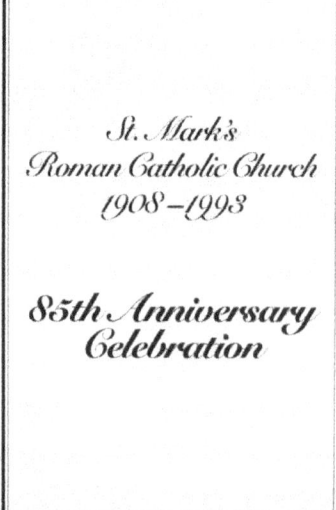

The Loving Legacy of Fr. Braun and Sr. Jeanne

St. Mark Church

Centennial Celebration for the Parish of St. Mark

September 27th, 2008

100th Anniversary

A Buffalo Scrapbook: St. Mark's Roman Catholic Parish

In the classroom at St. Mark

The wedding of Meg Lauerman and Mike Yeksigian, 1985

The Loving Legacy of Fr. Braun and Sr. Jeanne

A Buffalo Scrapbook: St. Mark's Roman Catholic Parish

Priest's gift a true sign of devotion
By Donn Esmonde, The Buffalo News, June 29, 2007

This is how it goes when your heart is unusually large.

This is how it goes when you devote your life to helping people, when your immediate and ultimate boss is God, when you live a life of generosity that, time and again, moves others to give more of themselves.

There was a picnic and fundraising raffle at St. Mark School last week. It is a small parish school -- about 300 students -- and church that bring hundreds of folks in the Delaware Park neighborhood into a loose extended family.

Survival is the goal and prosperity an illusion in a struggling diocese that is closing city schools and churches. Raffles and bake sales and candy drives fill the financial hole at St. Mark's that tuition and fees do not cover.

The big draw at Sunday's picnic, aside from the bounce house and grilled hot dogs, was a shot at a weeklong cruise or $2,000 cash. It was a big prize and a pricey ticket: 50 bucks. When the winning number was pulled, folks were perplexed. No name, just initials.

The mystery was quickly solved. The parish priest, Monsignor Francis Braun, bought $1,000 worth of tickets. He put the initials of different people on each, without telling any of them. Some were families he knew could not afford to take a cruise. Other initials were those of area service men -- some of them graduates of St. Mark's school, others with relatives or friends in the parish.

The winner was an Army officer from Ellicottville who recently returned from Iraq and now is stationed Washington, D.C. Braun met him nearly 10 years ago on an annual jaunt with friends to an Army football game at West Point. Braun's group always takes a bunch of local cadets to dinner, and the future officer was among them.

In the years that followed, he was among the local servicemen Braun and friends occasionally took to Bisons games. When filling out his $1,000 worth of tickets last week, the priest routinely put the officer's initials on one.

The Army officer -- whose name Braun asked I not print, given increasing opposition to the Iraq War -- won $2,000 in a contest he never knew he

The Loving Legacy of Fr. Braun and Sr. Jeanne

entered. Although Braun didn't have the officer's contact information when I wrote this, he expects to soon track the serviceman down with the good news.

Braun, 77, has been a priest since he was 24. He has a bum knee, a younger man's eyes and an ease with words. The bedrock of his generosity is not just faith, but the emotional pain that forms a soft heart. Some of his seminary school classmates were killed in Korea. Fifteen of the boys he taught in high school died in Vietnam. He spoke about the losses on a recent afternoon, sitting on a folding chair in a small office in the rectory.

"All of these people," he said, shaking his head, "dying in service to our country."

His weekly Sunday Mass includes prayers for 13 service people connected by membership or relation to the parish. Pictures of some of them hang in the halls of the school. Each class, in grades K through 8, adopts a service person every year. "They are stationed all over the world -- in Iraq, in Afghanistan, the Mediterranean," Braun said. "A lot of our kids know their families -- are friends with a younger brother or sister."

This is how it is in this and in countless other small parish communities. The absent are not forgotten. Those serving their country are honored. The hand of generosity extends. The kindness of spirit shows itself in prayers from a pulpit. It is seen in pictures on a school wall. Sometimes it even is revealed in initials written on a raffle ticket.

There are chances each of us, at various times, take in life. And there are rewards far larger than a winning ticket.

Above: Fr. Braun on the mic at Lionheart 2010

A Buffalo Scrapbook: St. Mark's Roman Catholic Parish

In honor of the 50th anniversary of his ordination, the St. Mark School gym was rededicated as "The Msgr. Francis Braun Auditorium"; a lasting commemoration set in stone which can't begin to reflect the feelings for our beloved Pastor Emeritus.

Msgr. Francis Braun retired as pastor of St. Mark in September, 2010.

The Loving Legacy of Fr. Braun and Sr. Jeanne

The following appeared in the St. Mark bulletin on September 19, 2010.

Farewell to our beloved pastor, Father Braun

Today, we stop to thank a great man for being such a beautiful servant of God to St. Mark's parishioners and school families for the past 30 years.

Fr. Braun has, in so many ways, been the watchful, guiding presence of Christ for our students, their families, our teachers and our community.

Year after year, he has lovingly welcomed our children into God's family in Baptism, given them God's forgiveness in Penance and fed them with the Body of Christ in the Eucharist. He has been a listening ear and source of wisdom for so many of our families.

His homilies helped us to live according to the teachings of Jesus in the Gospel. These homilies, whether telling us about the Bills, the Sabres, St. Mark or how proud we should be to live in the City of Buffalo, will never be forgotten.

Our children will miss he protective, caring presence watching over their safety as they entered and left school each day.

Words fall short in expressing our heartfelt gratitude to Fr. Braun for his dedication, his loving kindness, and his Christ-like presence at St. Mark's.

On your retirement, Fr. Braun, we offer this prayer that St. Francis used when his brothers went out to preach. It is an adaptation of the Priestly Prayer from the Book of Numbers:

The Lord bless and keep you!

The Lord let His face shine upon you and be gracious to you!

The Lord look upon you kindly and give you peace!

The Lord bless you!

A Buffalo Scrapbook: St. Mark's Roman Catholic Parish

Sister Jeanne Eberle, principal at St. Mark's Elementary School in North Buffalo, gets hugs from Ryan Becker, left, Samantha Whitman and Ryan Lakamp on Wednesday.

Principal leaves a loving legacy
By Phil Fairbanks, The Buffalo News, June 23, 2011

Kevin Spitler thinks his good friend, Sister Jeanne Eberle, would have made a great lawyer.

"The big law firms would love her," said Spitler, a well-known local attorney. "Her billable hours would be in the stratosphere."

In other words, Eberle, the principal of St. Mark's Elementary School in North Buffalo, may be the hardest-working educator around. And after 34 years at the helm of one of Buffalo's most successful academic programs, she's stepping down. A Mass in her honor will be offered at 9:15 a.m. today at St. Mark's, 399 Woodward Ave.

The Sisters of St. Joseph nun leaves with a legacy that has touched thousands of kids. It was her love of the individual child that got her up each morning and, more often than not, kept her working late at night.

The Loving Legacy of Fr. Braun and Sr. Jeanne

"She wanted every opportunity for her pupils to shine," said Frank Cecala, an English teacher at the school. "Her calling was to reach all children, and she did it in a unique and remarkable way."

Even now, 12 years after he joined St. Mark's, Cecala marvels at Eberle's insistence on sending handwritten Christmas cards to each of the school's 400 students and her practice of adding personal notes to their report cards.

"She believes everybody has a gift and you simply have to find a way to get it out," said Nancy Roberts, a former teacher at the school. "She also believes learning should be fun and wrapped in love."

Over the years, St. Mark's has gained a reputation as one of the most successful elementary and middle schools in the region.

And yet, despite standardized test scores that rival the best private and public schools around, Eberle will tell you that developing a relationship with kids is even more important than teaching them how to take a test.

Ask any of her close friends and chances are good you'll hear a story about an at-risk child who came to St. Mark's as an underachiever and left destined for success.

"I asked her at graduation this week, 'Who did you save this year?' " said Mary Elaine Spitler, a research scientist in the University at Buffalo's early education department. "One of Sister Jeanne's special characteristics is her ability to see the potential in every kid."

And those are the children she often talks about when asked about a legacy that stretches back 50 years. Eberle loves to tell the story of the second-grader who came to St. Mark's after getting expelled from another Catholic school.

Despite the urgings of others, she stuck by him, and today, he's a student in UB's medical school.

"I just want to be remembered for taking a special interest in kids," Eberle said. "The important thing is to develop a relationship with them by showing them love and compassion and giving them a reason to like school."

Leaving St. Mark's will be difficult. What will she miss most?

A Buffalo Scrapbook: St. Mark's Roman Catholic Parish

"I told one of our eighth-graders the other day, 'Do you think I like you?' " she said with a huge smile.

"I don't know," he answered.

A few days later, that same kid gave her a hug she'll never forget.

"I'll miss the hugs," she said.

And no doubt, so will the kids at St. Mark's.

Sr. Jeanne, same as always at her retirement party: Having a blast—with a warm smile and contagious laugh, and one of her "kids" on her arm.

The Loving Legacy of Fr. Braun and Sr. Jeanne

A Buffalo Scrapbook: St. Mark's Roman Catholic Parish

Bishop Edward Kmiec appointed Rev. Joseph S. Rogliano as the ninth pastor of St. Mark in September, 2010. At the same time, Fr. Joe was appointed pastor of St. Rose of Lima on Parker Avenue. His concurrent appointment at both parishes solidified the notion presented in the Diocesan "Journey of Faith and Grace," which "linked" the two still-separate parishes.

From his first week in North Buffalo, Fr. Joe began bringing the two parishes together in a variety of ways.

Immediately, weekday and weekend Masses began an alternating schedule between the two church buildings, with parishioners from both parishes welcome at any Mass.

Another early outward sign of the linking of the parishes was a joint bulletin.

200

The Loving Legacy of Fr. Braun and Sr. Jeanne

A Few Questions for Fr. Joe

You talk about your family a lot, and we see them here all the time. They seem like a fun group.

We're a very close family. That became even more true when my dad passed away unexpectedly at the age of 49 when as a family, we were getting ready for my sister's wedding.

Both of my parents were Italian, so you know there's that close emotional element. My sisters and I have all been blessed with a similar sense of humor, so we laugh through it all, especially our crises and heartache.

We're still a strong, close family. My sisters' kids are having kids, which can make it tough for all of us to get together. My family also knows the pain of divorce, which can sometimes add to the difficulty in all being together at the same place, but my family is my life. And that includes my extended family-- my friends and parishioners wherever I go.

I'm lucky that my family gets along. I'm lucky that my farthest sister is only 80 miles away, and that we really enjoy getting together. It's nice to get together, and really just let it rip with people you love.

What's been unique about your first four years at St. Mark?

Being the pastor of linked parishes with a school is unique. In Lockport, where I was pastor of linked parishes, the school was a regional school-- not a parish school like St. Mark where I have more responsibility. Having the two parishes, plus the historic and thriving school, makes it three separate entities which require a lot of my time.

Following a living legend like Fran Braun is different, too. I've followed long term, wonderful pastors before, great guys. But during the 30 years he spent here, Fran was simply beloved-- and beloved on a completely different level for a very, very long time.

The same is true with Sr. Jeanne. Working with a principal who was finishing out an amazing 34 year career was certainly unique, and it was a blessing to spend a year with her.

A Buffalo Scrapbook: St. Mark's Roman Catholic Parish

Maybe the most unique? (laughing.) When I moved in, I asked, "Where do I sleep?" Anywhere you'd like, was the response. "All the rooms have been painted." But there was no furniture. Anywhere. I was really excited to get in this big house and see all the rooms, but it was empty room after empty room. Beautifully painted, but empty. I didn't expect having to go furniture shopping my first week here, but it all worked out, especially since I wound up with exactly what I wanted—which may have been the plan, anyway.

The Loving Legacy of Fr. Braun and Sr. Jeanne

It's nothing you haven't heard before-- You're a different kind of priest, a different kind of guy. What makes you different?

I don't really consider myself *different*; I just have to be myself. My experience might be different from some guys; I didn't grow up heavily involved in the church. I didn't know what a breviary was when I got to the seminary. My call was based in a religious experience I had during a retreat at my home parish.

My thirtieth year as a priest is coming up. A lot of people said the odds were against me, but what I find supports my ministry and my life is, staying true to who I am. The more you meet people, if you relate to them, don't place yourself above them-- you have more of a connection with those people, and they feel more comfortable with you.

People are sometimes shocked to find out I'm a priest if they meet me out of context. I don't know if I break an image, if I smile too much... but I'm an extrovert who lives alone. So as an extrovert, when I'm around people, I like to make the most of it. I seem to connect with people who aren't your typical church goers at a restaurant or at the gym. The older I get, the more I feel like that's how God is using me. I can't exactly put my finger on it, but I feel like I have to embrace it.

Early in my priesthood, I tried much more to fit the mold. Now, I can be me. I feel like I'm in my prime. I can be more involved with the Diocese and Diocesan functions. I feel like it's one of my blessings of being here. We hosted a party for the priests of the Diocese at St. Mark's, and the Bishop looked at me and said, "You know, I think you get more out this than we do." He was right.

I really wake up every day grateful and happy, and I've never had a day in my priesthood where I was dreading the day. I have sometimes dreaded my schedule, or sometimes dread a particularly sad or difficult occasion or Mass.

Those days, I ask, "What are You doing with me? I know you want me here, but am I doing the right thing?"

I chuckle a lot when I talk to Him, because I'm affirmed when someone tells me that I knew exactly what they were thinking, and I made it so much clearer for them. Of course, most of the time, the truth is, I had no idea *exactly* what you were thinking. But that's the spirit. That's the grace. Those little things are a sign to me, which say "Keep on, keep at it, stay the course.

A Buffalo Scrapbook: St. Mark's Roman Catholic Parish

One of the most outward signs of change since Fr. Joe came to St. Mark was the addition of a handicapped entrance at the front of the church. Many of the activities started in recent years, like the annual golf tournament (brochure cover, right) and the "Crossing Hertel" Dance have been developed to bring St. Mark and St. Rose together, to benefit both parishes.

The Loving Legacy of Fr. Braun and Sr. Jeanne

A Buffalo Scrapbook: St. Mark's Roman Catholic Parish

While some things have changed, some have also stayed the same. Sr. Jeanne and Sr. Kathleen had returned to help produce the Christmas Eve Mass pageant. Below, Fr. Joe helps run the St. Mark Lionheart auction.

The Loving Legacy of Fr. Braun and Sr. Jeanne

Fr. Joe has continued the tradition of Masses for sports teams from school, as school faculty, staff, and parents have continued the tradition of volunteering at Dyngus Day celebrations in the Polonia district to bring in money for the school.

A Buffalo Scrapbook: St. Mark's Roman Catholic Parish

Long before Fr. Joe made his way to St. Mark, he was known as an "exercise freak." In fact, that was the exact phrase he used in a 1994 New York Times article about interesting people who have second jobs in health spas around the country. His story and photos were featured in The Times' Living Section while he was an assistant at St. Gregory the Great Parish.

From the New York Times, November 2, 1994

The Rev. Joseph S. Rogliano, a Roman Catholic priest in Buffalo, has been an aerobics instructor on the side for seven years. "In my parish, they know I'm an exercise freak," said the 37-year-old priest, who is listed on the roster of teachers at the Bally Matrix health club as Father Joe.

For the two classes he teaches each week -- one in the morning, the other in the evening -- Father Joe dresses in shorts and a T-shirt. "I put on whatever comes up in my drawer, and hopefully the socks don't have holes," he said.

He insists that becoming an exercise instructor "was not something that I was looking for." It all began when a friend persuaded him to take an aerobics class. "I had the typical male response: 'You're not going to get me in there, jumping around!' " he said. "After 20 minutes

The Loving Legacy of Fr. Braun and Sr. Jeanne

I had the other typical male reaction: I couldn't breathe." But now that he has reconditioned and recharged his body, he leads a very vigorous class where "we kick in high gear," he said.

Father Joe calls the health club his "second ministry," for he has counseled several of his students and has even performed their marriages. But he concedes that a health club "is an unlikely place for a priest -- it has an image as a place for single people to meet."

Photographs by Mike Groll for The New York Times

Above, the Rev. Joseph S. Rogliano, a Roman Catholic priest in Buffalo, teaching aerobics at the Bally Matrix health club. He calls the class, which he has taught for seven years, his "second ministry." Left, Father Rogliano at his church, St. Gregory the Great.

The music ministry at St. Mark has seen a rebirth in the time since Fr. Joe's arrival. We are blessed as a community to have many fine musicians who are regulars and semi-regulars at Masses at St. Mark and St. Rose.

The Loving Legacy of Fr. Braun and Sr. Jeanne

Causing trouble and making smiles: Fr. Joe does a beard check on Santa Jim Honer above. Below, the genuine article poses with two St. Mark students who dressed up as their pastor for Celebrity Day at school.

A Buffalo Scrapbook: St. Mark's Roman Catholic Parish

Fr. Joe & Fr. Tom at a "Crossing Hertel" party at St. Rose of Lima. Rev. Thomas Ribits, OSFS, is a weekend associate at both parishes.

Ribits a godsend for O'Hara art students
By Barbara Tucker, The Tonawanda News, December 19, 2013

Ever since he was a boy, the Rev. Thomas Ribits, OSFS, recalls his love of art — a passion that turned into his life's work.

A priest of the order of the Oblates of St. Francis deSales, Ribits grew up in Detroit, and for 24 years, taught elementary and high school students at Nardin Academy in Buffalo, then was campus minister at D'Youville College before taking a sabbatical to devote more attention to his art work.

Last year, he joined the faculty at Cardinal O'Hara High School in the Tonawanda to teach advanced art and religion. Known at O'Hara as "Father Tom," Ribits said he's enjoying the school and students.

"I find the kids are down to earth, with genuine care and concern for each other," Ribits said. His background extends from earning a degree in theology in Toronto to a master of arts from Buffalo State, drawing courses at the Detroit Institute of Art and taking other art courses along the way.

Ribits established the Salesian Studio in Buffalo, provided by his order, where he has his art studio. Among his many accomplishments are murals at St. Joseph's Cathedral in Buffalo and an enormous mural project at the Catholic Center in Buffalo.

"The mock-up for the (Catholic Center) mural took six months," he said. "'To finish the work took 13 months, working 50 to 60 hours a week, while teaching at the same time. I would work from 5 to 7 a.m., celebrate 7:30 a.m. Mass, then teach, returning to work on the mural from 3 to 9 p.m. — an all day project."

"I had a lot of energy," he laughed.

Mary Holzerland, principal at O'Hara, said when she first met Ribits, she knew he belonged at O'Hara, which she noted, has a tradition of a strong art program. "Last year, he assisted with Masses at the school and at the reconciliation services. He was, and is now, invaluable on a daily basis. We're fortunate to have two priest who minister to our kids."

Holzerland said Ribits offers students his intense passion for art — and holds them accountable. "In the classroom, he offers students a higher level of thinking, skills they need every day," she said. "Not all our students are Catholic and he helps each student to have a deeper understanding of God. He shares the kids' backgounds which helps them know each other. He's just really good."

At O'Hara, Ribits teaches two religion classes and a studio in art class for those who are really interested in art. "Art needs a lot of self-discipline. We work in acrylic — easier to clean up," he noted.

Outside of school and his art projects, Ribits enjoys hiking, biking and running. "In good weather, it's not unusual to see Father Tom riding his bike to school," Holzerland said.

In fact, the day of the interview was a "dress down" red and green day at the school to raise money to help four needy families on the West Side of Buffalo. Ribits came in dressed in red and green sweaters, with one red and one green sneaker. "I have a lot of sneakers," he laughed, "in fact I have another pair like this at home. I take one year at a time and live the present moment," he added.

A Buffalo Scrapbook: St. Mark's Roman Catholic Parish

Sr. Kathleen's retirement in 2012 meant the end of an era at St. Mark. She was the last of dozens of Sisters of St. Joseph to educate the children of St. Mark since 1921. When Sr. Jeanne retired in 2011, the school welcomed Lee Brenner as St. Mark's first lay principal. In 2014, Robert Clemens, the longtime principal at PS 81, became the first male principal in SMK's 92 years.

Principal Lee Brenner with Bishop Malone and St. Mark students who helped raise $12,500 for Catholic Charities.

The Loving Legacy of Fr. Braun and Sr. Jeanne

St. Mark School Principals

1921-28:	Sr. Martina Brown
1928-38:	Sr. Mary Grace Seefried
1938-45:	Sr. Jeanette Poulin
1945-46:	Sr. Sylvester Hurley
1946-49:	Sr. Kathleen McCann
1949-54:	Sr. Catherine McNeil
1954-57:	Sr. Margaret Scott (Sr. Maris Stella)
1957-63:	Sr. Mary Walter Love
1963-77:	Sr. Thomas Acquinas Lennon
1977-2011:	Sr. Jeanne Eberle (Sr. Joan of Arc)
2011-14:	Mrs. Lee Brenner
2014-	Mr. Robert Clemens

Sisters who taught at St. Mark

Sr. Kathleen Barrett, Sr. Rita Barrett, Sr. Marcella Bauerlein, Sr. M. Evangelista Bennion, Sr. Jane Boudreau, Sr. Raphael Brick, Sr. Rose Marie Brick, Sr. Eileen Britt (Sr. St. Edmund), Sr. M. Vincent de Paul Brogan, Sr. M. Harold Brown, Sr. Mary Anne Butler (Sr. Mary Jeanne)

Sr. Alice Callaghan (Sr. Margaret Ann), Sr. Mary Rene Connors, Sr. Joseph Mary Coughlin, Sr. M. Perpetua Cullen

Sr. M. Adele Daigler, Sr. Joseph Marie Debroske, Sr. Bette DiCesare (Sr. Paul Joseph), Sr. Patricia Durkin (Sr. Miriam), Sr. M. Theophane Dwyer

Sr. M. Mechtilde Engel

A Buffalo Scrapbook: St. Mark's Roman Catholic Parish

Sr. M. Loretta Fahey, Sr. Julia Feltz (Sr. Mary Ernest), Sr. Cecile Ferland, Sr. Beth Ann Finster, Sr. Catherine Flury (Sr. M. Edgar), Sr. M. Anita Fortune, Sr. Winifred Fox

Sr. Catherine Gallagher (Sr. Francis Xavier), Sr. M. Cassiana Gibbons, Sr. Joseph Damien Golden

Sr. Elizabeth Ann Harding (sr. Mary William), Sr. Ann Therese Hedges, Sr. Mary C. Henry (Sr. Liquori), Sr. Mary Helen Pope, Sr. Alice Huber (Sr. Mary Lawrence)

Sr. M Emmanuel Ibbotson

Sr. M. Victorine James, Sr. Robert Anne Jones, Sr. M. Concepta Joyce

Sr. Rita Kane (Sr. John Aloysius), Sr. St. Charles Keib, Sr. Marie Kerwin, Sr. Gertude Klein, Sr. Julia Agnes Koster, Sr. Maureen Krantz (Sr. St. Gregory), Sr. Monica Krupinski

Sr. Mary Edward Lamb, Sr. M. Pancratia Lamb, Sr. Delores Lavin, Sr. Nora Latourneau, Sr. Jane Catherine Lynch, Sr. Gerald William Long (Sr. Ellen Long)

Sr. Maryann Martin (Sr. Mary Karen), Sr. Bea Manzella, Sr. Anne Joachim McCarthy, Sr. Ellen McCarty (Sr. Elizabeth Ann), Sr. M. Francis Borgia McCormick, Sr. Theresa Marie McHugh, Sr. Carol McTigue (Sr. Mary Hugh), Sr. M. Joan of Arc McTigue, Sr. Leo Xavier Messmer, Sr. Carol Morgan (Sr. Mary Lourdes), Sr. Mary Morrissey (Sr. Mary Francis), Sr. M. Richard Miller

Sr. M. Eunice O'Conner, Sr. M. Dositheus O'Laughlin

Sr. M. St. Martin Peters, Sr. M. Hubert Pollard, Sr. Paul of the Cross Privitera

Sr. Marcelline Quinn

Sr. Mary Raynor (Sr. M. Dominica), Sr. M. Ignance Reamer, Sr. Annette Reap, Sr. M. St. Henry Reish, Sr, M. Clement Romance

Sr. M. Eucharista Sawken, Sr. Alphonse Marie Schreck, Sr. M. Albina Seitz, Sr. Karen Shaver (Sr. St. Michael), Sr. M. Romana Spurrell, Sr. Dominic Scanlon, Sr. Margaret Mary Stover, Sr. M. Francis Elizabeth Stetter, Sr. M. Nolasco Swinburne

Sr. Ruth Trautman (Sr. M. Florentine)

Sr. M. Edwards Waechter, Sr. Rose Ann Weter, Sr. Alice Williams

Sr. Rosina Young

Sr. Jean Marie Zirnheld, Sr. Laurentia Zogby

A Buffalo Scrapbook: St. Mark's Roman Catholic Parish

Pastors of St. Mark Church

1908-1928:	Bishop John J. McMahon
1928-1937:	Rev. Robert E. Walsh
1937-1942:	Msgr. Charles E. Duffy
1942-1952:	Bishop Joseph A. Burke
1953-1970:	Msgr. Eugene A. Loftus
1970-1975:	Msgr. William J. Grant
1975-1980:	Rev. Robert G. Ochs
1980-2010:	Msgr. Francis Braun
2010- :	Rev. Joseph S. Rogliano

Associates:

Rev. Martin Fell

Rev. Edmund Gibbons

Rev. John Shea

Rev. Francis Hendricks

Msgr. Francis Garvey

Rev. Joseph Hynes

Rev. John McNamera

Rev. Felix McCabe

Rev. Francis Cronin

Rev. John Boyle

The Loving Legacy of Fr. Braun and Sr. Jeanne

REVEREND
FRANCIS GARVEY

*Assistant Pastor of
St. Mark's*

REVEREND
FRANCIS HENDRICKS

*Assistant Pastor of
St. Mark's*

1933

A Buffalo Scrapbook: St. Mark's Roman Catholic Parish

Rev. Michael Gallagher

Rev. James Hayes

Rev Austin Crotty

Msgr. Edward Walker

Rev. Joseph Sekelsky

Rev. Raymond Herzing

Rev. John Culbert

Rev. Joseph Manger

Msgr. James Chambers

The Priest Staff at St. Marks

THE REVEREND
JOSEPH F. MAGNER, M.A.

THE REVEREND
JAMES F. CHAMBERS, S.T.L.

1954

The Loving Legacy of Fr. Braun and Sr. Jeanne

Rev. John McCarthy

Rev. Paul Durkin

Msgr. Robert Williamson

Msgr. Albert Clody

Msgr. John Madsen

Rev. Carl Kuehmeier

Rev. Dennis Mende

Rev. Ronald Mierzwa

Rev. Vincent Wright

Introducing Father Ron

Weekend Associates

Msgr. John J. Coniff

Msgr. Henry J. Gugino

Rev. Thomas Ribits, OSFS

A Buffalo Scrapbook: St. Mark's Roman Catholic Parish

About the Author

Steve Cichon and his wife Monica have been members of St. Mark since 2000, and were married by Msgr. Braun. Neither has ever felt more welcome in a parish than when they sat at Father's kitchen table to discuss their wedding. They knew this church and this priest were something special. Fifteen years later, they consider Msgr. Braun's friendship one of the greatest benefits of the quite accidental finding of their dream home in Parkside.

They both serve as Eucharistic Ministers at the 9:30 Mass and are one of the teams which conduct wedding rehearsals at St. Mark and St. Rose. Steve has also been a Lector since 2005, and was St. Mark Parish Council President 2012-13.

Steve is also related to Sr. Jeanne, who is his grandmother's first cousin. He sees the same devoted love in Sr. Jeanne that he saw in his grandmother, and calls the blessing of watching it shared among so many a blessing beyond words. Several years ago, when Steve inquired about a need for Religious Ed teachers, and Sr. Jeanne found out; she leapt out of her chair, wrapped her arms around his neck, and kissed him on the cheek. Feeling Sister's joy, there was really no way Steve *couldn't be a catechist* for the coming school year.

Mostly, Steve is just honored to be in a position to help commemorate two beautiful, amazing people in our lives.

The Loving Legacy of Fr. Braun and Sr. Jeanne

THANKS....

Mary Ann Moriarty

Doran & Murphy Attorneys at Law

Msgr. Francis Braun, Sr. Jeanne Eberle, Sr. Kathleen Barrett, Fr. Joe Rogliano, Dan Ryan, Megan Gallagher, Angela Pritchard, Mary Pat Littlefield, Chrissy Murphy, Meg Lauerman, Fr. Tom Ribits, Sr. Madonna Sweet, Sr. Patricia Reen, The Arthur Family, Laura Genco, Peter Bukowski, Fr. John Mack, Mary Dickerson, Kathy & Dick Gilbert, Jeanette Kinney Donovan, Dave Schank, Marcia Spitler, Anna Benson, Edmund Haremski, Kathleen Hourihan, all St. Mark School students and alumni, and all the parishioners past and present of St. Mark and St. Rose.

Marty Biniasz, Brian Meyer, Kevin Keenan, Patrick McPartland, John Bisci, Al Wallack, Michael and Mary O'Sullivan, Len Mattie, Nancy Abramo, Ruth & David Lampe, Michael Riester, Tom Ziobro, Rich Wolf, Peggy Milliron, Bernhard Wagner, Adam & Theresa Roma, Ron & Rosanne Wagner, Amber Small, Matthew Pelky, The Cichon, Coyle, Huxley and Martyna families, and, of course, my sweetie pie... Monica Cichon.

The author and Msgr. Braun head out to the 1812 memorial at the Delaware Park Golf Course, Memorial Day 2011.

A Buffalo Scrapbook: St. Mark's Roman Catholic Parish

ST. MARK...

Pray for us

www.ingramcontent.com/pod-product-compliance
Lightning Source LLC
Chambersburg PA
CBHW051916160426
43198CB00012B/1917

9780982873922